RENEWING WORSHIP

Holy Baptism

and Related Rites

Evangelical Lutheran Church in America
Published by Augsburg Fortress

RENEWING WORSHIP 3
Holy Baptism and Related Rites

*This resource has been prepared by the Evangelical Lutheran
Church in America for provisional use.*

The paper used in this publication meets the minimum re-
quirements of American National Standard for Information
Sciences—Permanence of Paper for Printed Library Materials,
ANSI Z329.48-1984.

Manufactured in the U.S.A. ISBN 0-8066-7002-9

06 05 04 03 02   1   2   3   4   5

Contents

Preface

In the years since the publication of *Lutheran Book of Worship* in 1978, the pace of change both within the church and beyond has quickened. The past three decades have seen not only a growing ecumenical consensus but also a deepened focus on the church's mission to the world. The church has embraced broadened understandings of culture, increasing musical diversity, changes in the usage of language, a renewed understanding of the central pattern of Christian worship, and an explosion of electronic media and technologies. These shifts have had a profound effect on the weekly assembly gathered around word and sacrament. The present situation calls for a renewal of worship and of common resources for worship, a renewal grounded in the treasures of the church's history while open to the possibilities of the future.

Renewing Worship is a response to these emerging changes in the life of the church and the world. Renewing Worship includes a series of provisional resources intended to provide worship leaders with a range of proposed strategies and materials that address the various liturgical and musical needs of the church. These resources are offered to assist the renewal of corporate worship in a variety of settings, especially among Lutheran churches, in anticipation of the next generation of primary worship resources.

Published on a semiannual basis beginning in 2001, this series includes hymns and songs (newly written or discovered as well as new approaches to common texts and tunes), liturgical texts and music for weekly and seasonal use, occasional rites (such as marriage, healing, and funeral), resources for daily prayer (morning prayer, evening prayer, and prayer at the close of the day), psalms and canticles, prayers and lectionary texts, and other supporting materials. Over the course of several years, worship leaders will have the opportunity to obtain and evaluate a wide range of Renewing Worship resources both in traditional print format and in electronic form delivered via the Internet at www.renewingworship.org.

These published resources, however, are only one component of the Renewing Worship multiyear plan led by the Evangelical Lutheran Church in America (ELCA) as it enters the next generation of its worship life. Endorsed by the ELCA Church Council and carried out in partnership by the ELCA Division for Congregational Ministries and the ELCA Publishing House (Augsburg Fortress), this plan for worship renewal includes five components. The first phase (2001–2002) is a consultative process intended to develop principles for language, music, preaching, and worship space. Related to *The Use of the Means of Grace,* the ELCA's statement on sacramental practices, the outcome of the 2001 consultative process has been published as *Principles for Worship*. These principles are intended to undergird future worship resource development and encourage congregational study, response, and practice.

The second phase (2001–2005) includes a series of editorial teams that collect, develop, and revise worship materials for provisional use. The liturgical and musical resource proposals that emerge from the editorial teams are being published during the third phase of this plan (also in 2001–2005) as trial-use resources in the Renewing Worship series, including the present volume, *Holy Baptism and Related Rites.* These materials include proposals for newly developed, ecumenically shared, or recently revised texts, rites, and music. Crucial to this phase will be careful evaluation and response by congregations and worship leaders based on these proposed strategies and provisional materials.

The fourth phase of the plan includes regional conferences for conversation, resource introduction and evaluation, and congregational feedback. The final phase of the process (2005 and beyond) envisions the drafting of a comprehensive proposal for new primary worship resources designed to succeed *Lutheran Book of Worship.*

As the plan progresses, the shape and parameters of that proposal will continue to unfold. The goal, however, will remain constant: renewing the worship of God in the church as it carries out Christ's mission in a new day.

Introduction

Holy Baptism and Related Rites is the first resource in the Renewing Worship series to focus on the primary patterns of the people of God as they gather for worship. The ongoing task of renewing worship appropriately begins with the sacrament of new birth. An insight dear to Lutherans, that baptism is not merely a onetime event but involves a daily dying and rising with Christ, applies also to worship renewal. The church comes again and again to the foundation of word and sacrament, to be renewed by them but also to renew its proclamation of the word and celebration of the sacraments in each new day.

This resource includes a provisional liturgy for baptism as it is celebrated in the primary Sunday assembly. Proposed materials are also included for rites that grow out of baptism: affirmation of baptism, and confession and forgiveness. Two additional sections outline processes for formation in faith related both to baptism and to affirmation of baptism. These sections reflect an emphasis on baptism as a lifelong journey of growth in faith that leads to the font and from it into the rest of life.

Renewing Worship resources have as one of their foundations *The Use of the Means of Grace,* the statement on the practice of word and sacrament adopted for guidance and practice by the Evangelical Lutheran Church in America in 1997.[1] This introduction includes highlights of that statement's guidance regarding baptism and briefly describes the contents of *Holy Baptism and Related Rites.*

BAPTISM IS A GIFT OF GOD

Whenever baptism is celebrated, the church reaches into its storehouse of images that proclaim what God is doing in this sacrament. Here are some of the central ways of saying what God is doing in baptism: "The triune God delivers us from the forces of evil, puts our sinful self to death, gives us new birth, adopts us as children, and makes us members of the body of Christ."[2] "Baptism inaugurates a life of discipleship."[3] "Individuals are baptized, yet this baptism forms a community."[4]

These and many other images, biblical stories, and theological formulations point to God as the one who acts in baptism. Baptism is a gift from God.

The gift of baptism comes to the church through Jesus Christ.[5] The church has grounded its teaching and practice about baptism in the great commission of Jesus to his followers: "Go therefore and make disciples of all nations, baptizing them in the name of the Father

---

[1] *The Use of the Means of Grace: A Statement on the Practice of Word and Sacrament* (Chicago: Evangelical Lutheran Church in America, 1997).

[2] *The Use of the Means of Grace,* principle 14.

[3] *The Use of the Means of Grace,* background 14A.

[4] *The Use of the Means of Grace,* application 14B.

[5] *The Use of the Means of Grace,* principle 15.

and of the Son and of the Holy Spirit, and teaching them to obey everything I have commanded you."[6] Jesus' own baptism by John and the way that Jesus spoke of his death on the cross as baptism[7] are also important to the church's understanding of baptism as gift. Christ draws a person into the water with him, where the Spirit comes and the baptized is named a beloved child of God. Christ joins the baptized to his death on the cross so that with Christ the baptized may be raised to new life.

Because the gifts of God are beyond measure, the gift of baptism is a gift for all.[8] The rite of baptism is broad and open enough to make it clear that baptism is for all ages: adults and older children who have been led to faith by the Holy Spirit and come to receive the gift of baptism, as well as younger children and infants brought to receive this gift by parents and sponsors who represent the whole community of faith. Because the gifts of God are beyond limit, the sacrament of baptism is enacted once in a person's life.[9] The church baptizes once for all time in order to proclaim the unfailing nature of God's promise, which is neither conditional nor vulnerable. The gift of baptism is one that can be continually returned to and reclaimed, but never needs to be reenacted. The rite of baptism and other related rites clearly distinguish between the once-for-all action of God in baptism and the occasions when the baptized affirm and remember that gift.

BAPTISM IS A WAY OF LIFE

The understanding of baptism as a singular event and gracious gift of God is balanced with an understanding of baptism as an ongoing way of life. Washing with water in the name of the triune God before the Christian assembly is at the center of one's whole life as a Christian, no matter when in life baptism occurs. The baptismal event is surrounded by a journey that includes nurture, formation, initiation, return, affirmation, remembrance, and ultimately the completion of God's promise in the life to come. The church's worship life includes a number of opportunities for marking the steps along this journey, and the primary liturgy of baptism itself holds together the gift of baptism and the life of the baptized.

The event of baptism is surrounded first of all by nurture and formation in the Christian faith. This lifelong process has a variety of patterns depending on when one comes to baptism. "When infants and young children are baptized, the parents and sponsors receive instruction and the children are taught throughout their development. With adults and older children, the baptismal candidates themselves are given instruction and formation for faith and ministry in the world both prior to and following their baptism."[10]

---

[6] Matthew 28:19.
[7] Luke 12:50; Mark 10:38.
[8] *The Use of the Means of Grace,* principle 18.
[9] *The Use of the Means of Grace,* principle 16.
[10] *The Use of the Means of Grace,* principle 19, application 19A.

Although congregations often expend considerable time and other resources on preparation for such occasions as marriage, first communion, confirmation, and even annual business meetings, they often overlook opportunities for a careful and fruitful period of preparation leading to the celebration of baptism. In the past this may have been due to an assumption that the vast majority of those to whom the church ministered knew the patterns and nuances of baptism.

The church is increasingly aware that there are many adults who come to church without having been evangelized or baptized, and that there are many parents who are struggling with the question of baptism for their children and seeking resources to help them. The last two decades have seen a renewal of the carefully structured, intentional model for baptismal formation known as the catechumenate, which has served the church well through the ages. This pattern, which includes teaching, prayer, and participation in the worship and mission of the community, not only prepares people for an event but also accompanies them into a life of discipleship. The process of nurture and formation clearly reveals that baptism is communal. Through baptism people are joined to the community of Christ. Parents, sponsors, catechists, mentors, and teachers walk with the candidate before and after baptism. The congregation as a whole participates through its various ministries of education and nurture.[11] A series of rites and prayers enables the worshiping assembly to voice its companionship with people who are being welcomed into the community of faith.

A second dimension of baptism as a way of life grows out of an insight championed by Martin Luther: "By God's gift and call, all of us who have been baptized into Christ Jesus are daily put to death so that we might be raised daily to newness of life."[12] Those who are baptized live in the reality that they are reborn children of God and at the same time subject to the brokenness of sin. A regular return to baptism, a daily dying and rising with Christ, is practiced in a variety of ways. Among these ways are confession and forgiveness, attending to the word of God, sharing in the eucharistic meal, daily prayer and the sign of the cross, the use of the catechism, and the profession of the creed. The church's worship life provides patterns for these practices, both corporate and individual. Throughout life, in one's return to baptism within the community of faith, God turns the baptized from the ways of sin and raises the baptized to new life in Christ.

In addition to these regular practices that return to baptism, affirmation of baptism is a third means of expressing baptism's significance for the whole of the Christian life. Rites for the affirmation of baptism enable the whole assembly to remember and be renewed in the gift of baptism, especially when celebrated at significant moments during the church year (such as the Vigil of Easter) or in connection with a congregational milestone.

---

[11] *The Use of the Means of Grace*, application 19B, principle 20.
[12] *The Use of the Means of Grace*, principle 17, based on The Small Catechism, The Sacrament of Holy Baptism, part four.

Affirmation of baptism may occur at significant points in the life of a baptized Christian, such as reception or restoration into membership of a congregation, or in connection with times of life passage and transition, such as youth confirmation, moving from the parental home, or retirement.[13]

Finally, because part of the gift of baptism is a commissioning for the mission of God, baptized people carry out that mission in their daily lives. All aspects of life are places where God's voice calls (*vocat*) the people of God to carry out their vocation, their calling. Christian vocation is more than an occupational choice, though it certainly is carried out in one's daily work. Christian vocation embraces the whole of life. Home and school, leisure and work, congregation and community, nation and world, citizenship and relationship, all belong to God and are places where the baptized carry out the commission to proclaim Christ, serve others, and strive for justice and peace.

THE CHRISTIAN ASSEMBLY CELEBRATES BAPTISM

The ways that Christian assemblies celebrate baptism and related rites proclaim both the unconditional gift of God's grace and the ongoing depth and richness of the life of the baptized. Attention to these rites and the practices and patterns surrounding them can help congregations "celebrate baptism in such a way that the celebration is a true and complete sign of the things which baptism signifies."[14]

▶   The primary weekly assembly of the congregation is the natural home for the celebration of baptism. The whole church, represented by the local community of faith and more specifically still by sponsors, plays a central role in welcoming and promising to support the newly baptized.[15] "An ordained minister presides . . . in the midst of a participating community."[16]

▶   Baptism has an integral place within the pattern of the assembly's worship, though that place may vary. Within the foundational pattern of gathering, word, meal, and sending, baptism after the proclamation of God's word emphasizes baptism's connection to faith in the promise of the gospel and leads the baptized to the eucharistic table. The baptism of infants as part of the gathering rite is an option that signifies the nature of baptism as entrance into the community where formation and nurture will follow.[17]

---

[13] *The Use of the Means of Grace,* principle 30, application 30A.
[14] *The Use of the Means of Grace,* principle 25. See Martin Luther, "The Holy and Blessed Sacrament of Baptism," I, in *Luther's Works,* volume 35 (Philadelphia: Fortress Press, 1965), 29.
[15] *The Use of the Means of Grace,* principle 21.
[16] *The Use of the Means of Grace,* principle 22.
[17] *The Use of the Means of Grace,* application 21B.

▶ Being washed in water in the name of the triune God is the essential center of the baptismal liturgy. This simple center, however, is more than perfunctory action and formulaic word. When the use of water is felt and seen and heard as genuine washing, when the words of the rite and the teaching surrounding it invite people into the fullness and power of God's very self—the name of the triune God—the baptismal liturgy is enriched.

▶ Generous physical signs underscore the meanings and importance of baptism, such as a font or water-pool of ample proportions visible to the assembly, the sight and sound of water used liberally, anointing with fragrant oil, clothing with a garment, the giving of candles lighted from the paschal candle to the newly baptized. Many of these signs refresh the assembly's connection to baptism even when the sacrament is not being celebrated: the font filled with water that may be touched when entering the assembly or approaching the table; the singing of a baptismal hymn or acclamation while water is scattered on the assembly; the paschal candle lighting up the days of Easter; the funeral pall clothing the faithful departed in the burial liturgy.[18]

▶ Finally, the practice of observing baptismal festivals across the course of the year has commended itself to many congregations as a way to heighten the celebration of baptism and its communal dimensions. In addition to the Vigil of Easter and the Day of Pentecost, All Saints Day and the Baptism of Our Lord are days that have dimensions of meaning that enrich the celebration of baptism.[19]

ONGOING DEVELOPMENT OF BAPTISMAL RITES

One of the chief goals toward which the Inter-Lutheran Commission on Worship worked in preparing the liturgy of *Lutheran Book of Worship* (*LBW*, 1978) was this one: "To restore to Holy Baptism the liturgical rank and dignity implied by Lutheran theology."[20] A quarter-century later, many signs suggest that this goal has been widely embraced among the churches that use *LBW* as a primary worship resource. Congregations have increasingly given the baptismal rite a prominent place in the principal worshiping assembly. The use of a unified rite for the baptism of infants and adults has both deepened the lifelong significance of infant baptism and reduced the perception that adult baptism is an unusual exception. Many resources for preaching, teaching and learning, congregational practice, and individual piety have emphasized themes of baptism within the whole of Christian life.

In the intervening years since *LBW*, other developments related to baptism and related rites have continued to occur.

---

[18] *The Use of the Means of Grace,* principles 26, 27, 28.
[19] *The Use of the Means of Grace,* application 25B.
[20] Introduction, *Lutheran Book of Worship,* 8.

There is a growing ecumenical convergence that recognizes one baptism as a principal sign expressing the unity of the church of Jesus Christ. The ecumenical consultations that led to *Baptism, Eucharist, and Ministry* (1982)[21] have led to further conversations seeking the mutual recognition of baptism.[22] A significant number of denominations have prepared revised baptismal rites since *LBW* appeared. Renewed Lutheran baptismal rites will reflect the gifts of the whole church as it works toward common understanding and expression of its unity.

There is a growing appreciation that the rite of baptism is at the center of a lifelong process of growth in Christ rather than being a singular act. Along with other Christians, Lutherans have been exploring these patterns of faith formation, as seen in the renewed interest in the adult catechumenate and in the preparation of materials such as Living Witnesses and Welcome to Christ.[23] Renewed Lutheran baptismal rites will provide for the church's needs as it celebrates the lifelong nurture and formation that accompany baptism.

There is a heightened focus on the relationship of baptism to mission. "Baptism and baptismal catechesis join the baptized to the mission of Christ."[24] The emphasis on baptism as individual salvation is increasingly balanced with an emphasis on baptism as initiation into the community of faith, a community that together renounces evil, proclaims the good news of Jesus Christ in word and deed, and strives for peace and justice in all the earth. Renewed Lutheran baptismal rites will reinforce the integral connection of baptism and the mission of Christ.

There is increasing sensitivity to the relationship of worship and culture. The Nairobi Statement of the Lutheran World Federation articulates well the transcultural, contextual, countercultural, and cross-cultural dimensions of this relationship.[25] Renewed Lutheran baptismal rites will affirm the common, transcultural core of the sacrament of baptism, while allowing for a variety of ways in which the practices surrounding baptism may reflect the contexts in which baptism is celebrated.

The following is a summary of the proposals in *Holy Baptism and Related Rites* that seek to respond to these ongoing developments.

---

[21] *Baptism, Eucharist and Ministry. Faith and Order Paper No. 111* (Geneva: World Council of Churches, 1982).

[22] A recent notable example: the consultations carried out by the Commission on Faith and Order of the World Council of Churches, resulting in the document "One Baptism: Towards Mutual Recognition of Christian Initiation," Faverges, France, October 2001.

[23] Living Witnesses: The Adult Catechumenate is a series of resources developed by the Evangelical Lutheran Church in Canada and released beginning in 1992. Welcome to Christ is a series of resources authorized by the Evangelical Lutheran Church in America and the Evangelical Lutheran Church in Canada for provisional use beginning in 1997.

[24] *The Use of the Means of Grace,* background 51A.

[25] "Nairobi Statement on Worship and Culture" in *Christian Worship: Unity in Cultural Diversity,* edited by S. Anita Stauffer (Geneva: Lutheran World Federation, 1996).

RENEWING WORSHIP: FOUNDATIONAL PATTERNS, FLEXIBLE RITES

Each of the provisional rites in this volume offers both a foundational pattern for the rite and a number of resources that can be used in flexible ways to fill out the rite within particular seasons and contexts. The rites are accompanied by narrative descriptions of their structure ("Shape of the Rite" or "Shape of the Process") and outlines of the elements of the rites. Primary or core elements of the rite are designated by boldface letters, together with supportive elements of the rite in regular type.

Some of the rites include alternatives within the body of the rites, which are further expanded with a section of supplemental texts. Marginal notes refer the user to the page numbers of the corresponding supplemental texts. This presentation—the essential shape of the rite, the core liturgy with texts and instructions, and a collection of supplemental texts—is intended to enrich and expand the celebration of these rites without obscuring what is central. Rites can be simple, transparent, accessible, and at the same time offer great variety and flexibility.

Pastoral circumstances often require the combination or adaptation of elements of the baptism and affirmation rites to respond to the needs of people who are participating in them (for example, the baptism of an infant coupled with the baptismal affirmation of the infant's parents as part of reception into membership). Although some suggestions are made here for such adaptation, more detailed guidance is beyond the scope of this provisional resource.

RENEWING WORSHIP: ONE BAPTISM, A LIFELONG PROCESS

The provisional rites in this volume reflect an understanding that baptism has the dual character of being at one and the same time a once-in-a-lifetime event and an ongoing way of life. These materials, therefore, include the primary rite of baptism, rites associated with formation in baptismal faith, rites associated with the periodic affirmation of the baptismal faith, and rites associated with the regular return to baptism through corporate confessional rites. (Other rites involving life passages such as marriage and funeral, which also have deep connections to baptism, will be presented in subsequent volumes in the Renewing Worship series.)

RENEWING WORSHIP: HOLY BAPTISM

The provisional liturgy for baptism presented here carries forward the essential aspects of the baptismal liturgy in *LBW*. Several additional developments may be noted.

▶ The *presentation* of candidates for baptism underscores the unitary character of the rite of baptism that is used with candidates of all ages. Various brief introductions to the rite are offered as options. The presentation includes a statement of commitment by the candidates, by sponsors, and by the whole assembly.

▶ The *profession* is located in closer proximity to the statements of commitment included in the presentation. In addition to a renunciation of evil, the profession includes an expression of the candidate's determination to be joined with Christ in baptism.

▶ The *thanksgiving* over the water of baptism is located in closer proximity to its actual use in the rite. In addition to a general prayer of thanksgiving, several seasonal prayers are offered that reinforce images associated with the Baptism of Our Lord, the Vigil of Easter, the Day of Pentecost, and All Saints Day.

▶ The *intercessory prayers,* which would normally include petitions for the newly baptized, parents, sponsors, and families, are here placed after the conclusion of the baptismal rite.

▶ The *welcome,* which may include the presentation of a lighted candle, is intended to strengthen the connection of baptism and the sending of the Christian community to carry out Christ's mission.

RENEWING WORSHIP: FORMATION IN FAITH RELATED TO BAPTISM

The second section of provisional rites in this volume is intended for use in the church's ministry of teaching and formation with those who are exploring the Christian faith and preparing for baptism. These rites enable the congregation to accompany such persons and to mark with them important milestones in a journey of discovery and conversion to Christ.

The rites included here are those that have been recently authorized for provisional use in the Evangelical Lutheran Church in America and the Evangelical Lutheran Church in Canada. They were published in the Welcome to Christ series in 1997.[26] They are incorporated into this volume so that they may be seen in the larger context of rites relating to baptism and so that they may receive additional feedback and response. They are best understood and used, however, as an integral part of the more comprehensive process of exploration and formation described in the Welcome to Christ series.

▶ *Welcome of Inquirers.* After a period of initial exploration and study, those who are inquiring into Christian faith and life may be welcomed into a period of deeper reflection on the Christian faith through the reading of scripture, prayer, worship, and ministry in daily life. This period of time has been historically known as the catechumenate.

---

[26] *Welcome to Christ: Lutheran Rites for the Catechumenate* (Minneapolis: Augsburg Fortress, 1997).

▶ *Enrollment of Candidates for Baptism.* Near the conclusion of the time of study and reflection, those who desire to be baptized publicly express that intention through this rite of enrollment. They then enter a time of final baptismal preparation, which is typically about six weeks in length, often coinciding with the season of Lent. Candidates are baptized and welcomed to the table at the Vigil of Easter or another of the chief baptismal festivals.

▶ *Blessing of Candidates.* So that the community of faith may accompany the candidates in their final preparations for baptism, blessings and prayers may be offered on the Sundays preceding baptism.

▶ *Affirmation of Christian Vocation.* At an appropriate interval after baptism, this rite of baptismal affirmation may be celebrated, during which the newly baptized affirm their vocation in the world. When baptism occurs at the Vigil of Easter, the Day of Pentecost is a fitting time for this affirmation.

▶ It is important to emphasize that these provisional rites for public celebration are only one component of the process of inquiry and formation surrounding baptism. Scripture, prayer, and ministry in daily life are other primary disciplines.

An additional area related to formation in faith that is not included here involves resources for preparing parents and sponsors who present infants and young children for baptism. This important dimension of baptismal preparation remains under development for future resources.

RENEWING WORSHIP: AFFIRMATION OF BAPTISM

The third section of this volume presents several rites for the affirmation of baptism. Congregations that use *LBW* have employed its Affirmation of Baptism rite with youth and adults as part of a ministry of teaching and formation, with those who are beginning membership in a Lutheran congregation after moving from another congregation or after a time away from the church, and with the entire worshiping assembly on particular occasions as a reaffirmation of baptismal promises. Some congregations have made further use of this rite or its essential shape with small group ministries and with individuals at times of life passage or in the context of counseling.

The rites presented here continue the basic pattern of the *LBW* rite. Several additional developments may be noted.

▶ The *shape of the rite* underscores the flexibility of a rite that often needs to be adapted to a wide range of congregational and personal circumstances.

▶ Rites for *public profession of faith, confirmation,* and *affirmation of baptism by the assembly* provide for a number of occasions that congregations frequently encounter.

▶ The *intercessory prayers,* which would normally include petitions for those affirming baptism, sponsors, and families, are here placed after the conclusion of the affirmation rite.

▶ The *prayer of blessing* may be accompanied by the laying on of hands. Laying on of hands is a powerful physical gesture of blessing that need not be restricted to particular uses of the affirmation rite.

▶ The *participation of the assembly* is reinforced through additional questions addressed to the assembly and through an acclamation at the conclusion of the rite, which may include the involvement of the assembly in a gesture or action that is a reminder of baptism.

Affirmation of Baptism is a versatile rite that supports the church in giving expression to the ongoing significance of baptism in the lives of Christian people. The baptized are renewed in the blessings associated with baptism, and with the guidance and help of the Holy Spirit they commit themselves again to the mission into which baptism sends them. Although a primary use of the rite may continue to be with young adults baptized in childhood who are making a profession of faith (confirmation), its more frequent use on other occasions, in connection with significant junctures in the lives of individual people and of the community of faith, will help to counter the impression that affirmation is a kind of unrepeatable graduation from one category of Christian identity to another.

The Use of the Means of Grace contains the beginnings of a list of such potential occasions: "Moving into a nursing home, beginning parenthood or grandparenthood, choosing or changing an occupation, moving out of the parental home, the diagnosis of a chronic illness, the end of one's first year of mourning, . . . retirement, . . . adoption and the naming of an already baptized child, release from prison, reunion of an immigrant family, and new life after abuse or addiction."[27] Additional provisional resources for a number of specific life passages will be included in subsequent volumes of Renewing Worship, but it is important to note the usefulness of Affirmation of Baptism as a starting point for rites that are helpful and powerful in many such situations.

RENEWING WORSHIP: FORMATION RELATED TO AFFIRMATION OF BAPTISM

The fourth section of this volume provides materials, similar in nature to those described in the second section, which may be used by the congregation with those who are coming to the affirmation of their baptism. They are based on those included in the resource *What Do You Seek?*[28] and are intended for use primarily with youth and adults who have been baptized at some point in their lives but wish to participate in a process of inquiry and formation leading to the affirmation of baptism.

---

[27] *The Use of the Means of Grace,* application 30A.
[28] *What Do You Seek?: Welcoming the Adult Inquirer* (Minneapolis: Augsburg Fortress, 2000).

RENEWING WORSHIP: CONFESSION AND FORGIVENESS

Martin Luther notes the integral relationship of baptism to confession and forgiveness: "Here you see that baptism, both by its power and by its signification, comprehends also the third sacrament, formerly called penance, which is really nothing else than baptism."[29] The fifth section of this volume presents a number of rites through which the assembly returns to baptism on a more regular basis than through affirmation rites, as Christians confess their sin and embrace the gift of forgiveness, often in connection with the primary weekly liturgy.

Rites of confession and forgiveness have included individual confession or reconciliation involving a confessor and a penitent, reconciliation involving individual relationships in need of healing, extended orders of corporate confession and forgiveness at particular times during the church year (such as Ash Wednesday) or in the context of communal brokenness or guilt, and brief general orders of corporate confession and forgiveness. The provisional rites in this volume are intended for use with the gathered assembly. Several features may be noted.

▶ The rites employ a *wider range of images and metaphors* for confession and forgiveness. Sometimes confessional rites have used a rather narrow range of juridical language: guilt, sin, forgiveness, justification. Scripture and Christian tradition offer many other images that can be used to expand upon these fundamental concepts: brokenness and healing, fragmentation and reconciliation, despair and hope, to name a few. Confessional rites need to encompass not only individual sin but also systemic, societal evil. Confessional rites also need to make room somehow for the participation of those who are victims of individual wrongdoing or communal oppression. A fuller collection of forms for confession and forgiveness can help to provide options for various circumstances, in addition to reinforcing seasonal themes throughout the church year.

▶ *Connections to baptism* are strengthened in these rites. The corporate form of confession and forgiveness includes an option for a baptismal reminder. Language of the brief general order includes baptismal themes and images. A brief order for the remembrance of baptism is offered as a possible replacement for an order for confession and forgiveness in the Sunday assembly, especially during the Easter season.

Although a rite of confession and forgiveness is neither an essential component of the Sunday liturgy nor a prerequisite for participation in holy communion, many Christians express the desire to acknowledge sin and brokenness on a fairly regular basis and to receive the assurance of God's steadfast love in forgiving word and baptismal water. Thus congregations continue to seek brief general confessional rites that speak with honesty

---

29 The Large Catechism, *The Book of Concord*, ed. Robert Kolb and Timothy J. Wengert (Minneapolis: Fortress Press, 2000), 465–6.

and grace. Although extended corporate confessional rites may not be as widely used, the pattern and examples presented here may suggest to congregations ways in which they can expand the opportunities to seek and embrace the mercy of God.

BAPTISM AT THE HEART OF CONGREGATIONAL RENEWAL

Renewing Worship is concerned not only with the revision and development of the church's liturgical forms, but above all with the renewal of the church through the gifts of God in the means of grace, the center of the church's life of worship. Many congregations are experiencing new life through a renewed understanding of baptism as a gift for the lifelong journey of both individual and community, and through practices and patterns that place baptism at the heart of worship, teaching and learning, and mission. As congregations embrace a rich and gracious theology and practice of baptism, seekers are led to the welcoming waters of baptism, the newly initiated are led to discipleship, the disciples are led to a fuller participation in the body of Christ, the body of Christ extends itself into the world, and all the baptized rediscover the treasures of returning to baptism again and again.

USING THIS RESOURCE

This collection is intended for provisional use among congregations of the Evangelical Lutheran Church in America and beyond. Worship leaders are encouraged to consider a congregation's history and worship practices before introducing new materials.

Materials in this collection are designed for provisional use in worship. Electronic files of selected materials are also available for download (www.renewingworship.org) and placement in congregational worship folders.

QUESTIONS OF COPYRIGHT

As a whole, the texts and arrangement of materials in *Holy Baptism and Related Rites* are covered under copyright (although individual items may be in the public domain or used here by arrangement with other publishers).

Permission is granted to reproduce copies for local onetime, congregational use between June 1, 2002 and December 31, 2005. Information regarding this provision and the required copyright notice is included on page ii of this resource.

EVALUATION

An essential goal of Renewing Worship is the evaluation of strategies and content proposals by worshiping congregations and their leaders. Included in each printed volume as well as on the website (www.renewingworship.org) is an evaluation form that addresses the strategies employed in each volume of the series. Feedback received will help to shape the subsequent stages of the process toward new worship materials.

Holy Baptism

Shape of the Rite

The pattern for the celebration of Christian baptism has a simple yet profound center: washing in water and speaking the word of God. From this center the pattern unfolds to include a gracious presentation of those to be baptized, the public profession of the faith of the church, other visible signs that amplify the meaning of baptism, and a welcome into the community of faith. Baptism is celebrated within the larger pattern of the Christian assembly's gathering around the word of God and the eucharistic meal. The powerful event of baptism in the assembly takes place within a larger pattern of formation in the faith, a lifelong process of discipleship.

PRESENTATION
Introduction
Presentation

The presiding minister may introduce the rite with a brief instruction about baptism, accenting themes that are developed elsewhere through scripture readings, preaching, music, and teaching. Sponsors who present candidates for baptism are baptized Christians who play a nurturing role in candidates' lives and who pledge to provide spiritual support in the future. Ordinarily such sponsors will be active participants in the life of the church, and it is advisable that at least one sponsor be a member of the congregation in which baptism occurs. The presentation includes statements expressing the mutual accountability of the baptized, the sponsors and parents, and the whole Christian community. These responses reveal that the baptized are united with and surrounded by an assembly gathered by the grace of God, people who rely on that grace to support one another in their commitments.

PROFESSION
Renunciation of Evil
Profession of Faith

The rite of baptism makes clear that baptism involves turning away from all that opposes God and turning one's allegiance to the triune God. Because Christ has first defeated every evil power, those to be baptized are freed and empowered to renounce all evil. Because they have been called and led to faith by the Holy Spirit, those coming to baptism are freed and empowered to turn to Christ, in the faith that is itself God's gift. The candidates' simple declaration of commitment to Christ is followed immediately by the profession of faith of the whole church. In solidarity with the candidates and as a sign of the ongoing renewal of baptism, the assembly joins in publicly declaring the faith. Ecumenical creeds join those to be baptized with the Christian community across time and space. The trinitarian profession of faith also anticipates baptism in the name of the triune God.

Central elements of the rite are noted in bold letters. Other elements support and reveal the essential shape of the rite.

BAPTISM
Thanksgiving
Baptism
Laying On of Hands
Signing with the Cross
Clothing with a Garment

The presiding minister gathers the thanksgiving of the whole assembly into a prayer that blesses God for the gift of water, recalls significant events in the story of salvation in which water is a sign of God's deliverance, and prays for the blessing of the Holy Spirit upon the water and those to be baptized in it. Baptism is not an isolated event; rather, it is connected to all of God's great actions in creating, redeeming, and enlivening the world.

The threefold washing with water in the triune name of God is essential to the liturgy of baptism. This is where utter dependence on the grace of God is most clearly revealed. All the baptized must be washed *by* someone else: it is a gift that may only be received. The gift is nothing less than life itself, for in this water a person dies with Christ and is raised by God to life in Christ.

The laying on of hands underscores what happens in baptism and gives thanks for God's presence in the newly baptized. The accompanying prayer asks that the gifts of the Holy Spirit, poured out on the baptized in the baptismal washing, continue to sustain and strengthen the life of the believer. The sign of the cross on the forehead is an ancient symbol that the newly baptized has also become united to Christ's death and resurrection. Anointing with oil, a biblical sign of being called and anointed by God, may be used to further signify that each Christian is joined to the mission of God.

Being clothed in a new garment reflects, at one level, a gracious response to a human need: after bathing, one needs to have clean and dry clothes. The symbolism connected with this garment is that in baptism Christ fully enfolds each believer: all who are baptized into Christ have put on Christ. This symbol is echoed at the end of life when the clothing of a funeral pall is used to cover the coffin of a Christian who has died.

WELCOME
Presentation of a Candle
Welcome

Presenting the newly baptized with a candle lighted from the congregation's paschal candle invites the newly baptized to join the community of faith in the mission of Christ. Walking in the light of God's pathways is both a delight and a duty. The congregation's active role in the welcome announces that the newly baptized have entered fully into the body of Christ, the household of faith. Every baptism enlarges the whole church on earth and contributes to the fulfillment of the great commission by Christ to the church (Matthew 28:19).

HOLY BAPTISM

Outline

PRESENTATION
Introduction
Presentation

PROFESSION
Renunciation of Evil
Profession of Faith

BAPTISM
Thanksgiving
Baptism
Laying On of Hands
Signing with the Cross
Clothing with a Garment

WELCOME
Presentation of a Candle
Welcome

HOLY BAPTISM

PRESENTATION

Candidates for baptism, sponsors, and parents gather with the ministers at the font.

INTRODUCTION

The presiding minister may address the assembly in these or similar words:

A p. 11 ▶

God, who is rich in mercy and love, gives us a new birth into a living hope through the sacrament of baptism. The power of sin is put to death in this holy flood, and we are raised with Jesus Christ to new life. We are united with all the baptized in the one body of Christ, anointed with the gift of the Holy Spirit, and sent out in mission for the life of the world.

PRESENTATION

One or more sponsors for each candidate, in turn, present the candidates:
I present *name* for baptism.

The presiding minister addresses candidates who are able to answer for themselves:
Name, trusting in the grace and love of God,
do you desire to be baptized?
Each candidate responds: I do.

The presiding minister addresses parents of children who are not able to answer for themselves:
Trusting in the grace and love of God,
do you desire to have your *children* baptized?
Response: I do.

The presiding minister may also address parents:

A p. 11 ▶

As you present your *children* for baptism,
you are entrusted with gifts and responsibilities:
to live with *them* among God's faithful people,
bring *them* to the word of God and the holy supper,
and nurture *them* in faith and prayer,
so that *they* may learn to trust God,
proclaim Christ through word and deed,
care for others and the world God made,
and work for justice and peace among all people.
Name/s, do you promise to help your *children* grow
in the Christian faith and life?
Response: I do.

The presiding minister addresses sponsors:

A p. 11 ▶

Sponsors, do you promise to nurture *these persons*
in the Christian faith as you are empowered by God's Spirit,
and to help *them* live in the covenant of baptism
and in communion with the church?
Response: I do.

The presiding minister addresses the assembly:
People of God, do you promise to support <u>*name/s*</u>
and pray for *them* in *their* new life in Christ?
We do.

PROFESSION

RENUNCIATION OF EVIL

The presiding minister addresses candidates and the parents and sponsors of young children:

A	B
I ask you to reject sin,	I ask you to reject sin,
profess your faith in Christ,	profess your faith in Christ,
and confess the faith of the church.	and confess the faith of the church.

p. 12 ▶

A

Do you renounce the devil
   and all the forces that defy God,
the powers of this world
   that rebel against God,
and the ways of sin
   that draw you from God?
Response: I do.

B

Do you renounce the devil
   and all the forces that defy God?
Response: I renounce them.

Do you renounce the powers of this world
   that rebel against God?
Response: I renounce them.

Do you renounce the ways of sin
   that draw you from God?
Response: I renounce them.

PROFESSION OF FAITH

The presiding minister may also ask the candidates and the parents and sponsors of young children:

A	B

Do you turn to Christ
   as your Lord and Savior?
Response: I do.
	Do you turn to Christ
	   as your Lord and Savior?
	Response: In faith I turn to Christ.

The presiding minister addresses the assembly:
With the whole church, let us confess our faith.

A
p. 12 ►

Do you believe in God the Father?
**I believe in God, the Father almighty,
creator of heaven and earth.**

Do you believe in Jesus Christ, the Son of God?
**I believe in Jesus Christ, God's only Son, our Lord,
who was conceived by the Holy Spirit,
born of the virgin Mary,
suffered under Pontius Pilate,
was crucified, died, and was buried;
he descended to the dead.
On the third day he rose again;
he ascended into heaven,
he is seated at the right hand of the Father,
and he will come to judge the living and the dead.**

Do you believe in God the Holy Spirit?
**I believe in the Holy Spirit,
the holy catholic church,
the communion of saints,
the forgiveness of sins,
the resurrection of the body,
and the life everlasting. Amen.**

BAPTISM

THANKSGIVING

Water may be poured into the font before or during the thanksgiving.

Standing at the font, the presiding minister begins the thanksgiving:
The Lord be with you.
And also with you.

Let us give thanks to the Lord our God.
It is right to give our thanks and praise.

A
pp. 13–18 ▶
We give you thanks, O God,
for in the beginning your Spirit brooded over the waters
and you created the world by your Word,
calling forth life in which you took delight.

Through water you led your people Israel
from slavery in Egypt to freedom in the promised land.
In the waters of the Jordan
Jesus was baptized by John and anointed with the Holy Spirit.
By the baptism of Jesus' death and resurrection
you delivered us from the power of sin and death
and set us free to live in you.

Send your Holy Spirit upon this water
and upon *all* who *are* washed in it,
that *they* may be given new life.
To you be given honor and praise
through Jesus Christ our Lord,
in the unity of the Holy Spirit, now and forever.
Amen.

BAPTISM

A
p. 18 ▶
The candidate is immersed into the water, or water is poured on the candidate's head, as the presiding minister says:
<u>Name</u>, I baptize you in the name of the Father,
The candidate is immersed, or water is poured on the candidate's head a second time:
and of the Son,
The candidate is immersed, or water is poured on the candidate's head a third time:
and of the Holy Spirit.
Amen.

The assembly may also respond with one of the following or another appropriate acclamation:

A

B

p. 18 ►

You belong to Christ,
in whom you have been baptized.
Alleluia.
Alleluia.

Blessed be God,
the source of all life,
the word of salvation,
the spirit of mercy.

LAYING ON OF HANDS

The presiding minister continues:
Let us pray.
We give you thanks, O God,
that through water and the Holy Spirit
you give your daughters and sons new birth,
wash them from sin, and raise them to eternal life.
The presiding minister lays both hands on the head of each newly baptized person and prays for each:
Sustain *name* with the gift of your Holy Spirit:
the spirit of wisdom and understanding,
the spirit of counsel and might,
the spirit of knowledge and the fear of the Lord,
the spirit of joy in your presence,
both now and forever.
Amen.

SIGNING WITH THE CROSS

The presiding minister marks the sign of the cross on the forehead of each of the baptized.
Oil prepared for this purpose may be used. As the sign of the cross is made, the minister says:
Name, child of God,
you have been sealed by the Holy Spirit
and marked with the cross of Christ forever.
Amen.

CLOTHING WITH A GARMENT

The newly baptized may receive a baptismal garment. The following words may also be said:
You have been clothed in Christ.
All who are baptized into Christ have put on Christ.

WELCOME

PRESENTATION OF A CANDLE

A lighted candle may be given to each of the newly baptized (to a sponsor of a young child) as a representative of the congregation says:
A   *p. 18* ▶
Walk in the faith of Christ crucified and risen.
Shine with the light of Christ.

WELCOME

The ministers and the baptismal group face the assembly. A representative of the congregation welcomes the newly baptized in these or similar words:
Through baptism you have been received into the household of God,
entrusted with the good news of Jesus Christ,
and strengthened to serve by the holy and life-giving Spirit.

The assembly may also offer a welcome in these or similar words:
We welcome you into the body of Christ
and the mission we share.
Join us as we give praise to God
and bear God's creative and redeeming word to all the world.

Those who have gathered at the font may return to their places. A psalm or hymn may be sung.

Supplemental Materials

The following texts may be used as alternatives to those included in the body of the rite.

INTRODUCTION

B

In baptism God frees us from sin and death by uniting us to the death and resurrection of Jesus Christ. Through water and the Holy Spirit we are reborn children of God, we are made members of the church, the body of Christ, and we are commissioned for Christ's ministry of justice and peace.

C

In holy baptism our gracious heavenly Father liberates us from sin and death by joining us to the death and resurrection of our Lord Jesus Christ. We are born children of a fallen humanity; in the waters of baptism we are reborn children of God and inheritors of eternal life. By water and the Holy Spirit we are made members of the church which is the body of Christ. As we live with him and with his people, we grow in faith, love, and obedience to the will of God.

PRESENTATION

Question to Parents

B

In Christian love you have presented *these children* for baptism. Do you promise to bring *them* faithfully to the services of God's house, teach *them* the Lord's Prayer, the Creed, and the Ten Commandments, place in *their hands* the Holy Scriptures, and provide for *their* instruction in the Christian faith, that, living in the covenant of *their* baptism and in communion with the church, *they* may lead *godly lives* until the day of Jesus Christ? *Response:* I do.

PRESENTATION

Question to Sponsors

B

In Christian love you have presented *these candidates* for baptism. Do you promise to care for *them* faithfully in every way as God gives you opportunity, that *they* may bear witness to the faith we profess, and that, living in the covenant of *their* baptism and in communion with the church, *they* may lead *godly lives* until the day of Jesus Christ? *Response:* I do.

RENUNCIATION OF EVIL

C

Through baptism we are called out of darkness into God's marvelous light.
To follow Christ means dying to sin and rising to new life with him.

Therefore I ask:
Do you reject the devil and all rebellion against God?
Response: I reject them.

Do you renounce the deceit and corruption of evil?
Response: I renounce them.

Do you repent of the sins that separate us from God and neighbor?
Response: I repent of them.

PROFESSION OF FAITH

B

Do you believe in God, the Father almighty,
creator of heaven and earth?
I believe.

Do you believe in Jesus Christ, God's only Son, our Lord,
who was conceived by the Holy Spirit,
and born of the Virgin Mary,
who suffered under Pontius Pilate,
was crucified, died, and was buried;
who descended to the dead,
and on the third day rose again;
who ascended into heaven,
and is seated at the right hand of the Father,
who will come to judge the living and the dead?
I believe.

Do you believe in the Holy Spirit,
the holy catholic church,
the communion of saints,
the forgiveness of sins,
the resurrection of the body,
and the life everlasting?
I believe.

THANKSGIVING

B

Holy God, mighty Lord, gracious Father:
We give you thanks, for in the beginning
your Spirit moved over the waters
and you created heaven and earth.
By the gift of water you nourish
and sustain us and all living things.
Blessed be God now and forever.

By the waters of the flood
you condemned the wicked
and saved those whom you had chosen,
Noah and his family.
You led Israel by the pillar of cloud and fire through the sea,
out of slavery into the freedom of the promised land.
Blessed be God now and forever.

In the waters of the Jordan
your Son was baptized by John and anointed with the Spirit.
By the baptism of his own death and resurrection
your beloved Son has set us free from the bondage to sin and death,
and has opened the way to the joy and freedom of everlasting life.
He made water a sign of the kingdom and of cleansing and rebirth.
In obedience to his command, we make disciples of all nations,
baptizing them in the name of the Father, and of the Son,
and of the Holy Spirit.
Blessed be God now and forever.

Pour out your Holy Spirit,
so that *those* who *are* here baptized may be given new life.
Wash away the sin of *all those* who *are* cleansed by this water
and bring *them* forth as *inheritors* of your glorious kingdom.
To you be given praise and honor and worship
through your Son, Jesus Christ our Lord,
in the unity of the Holy Spirit, now and forever.
Amen.

C

Eternal and gracious God, we give you thanks.
In countless ways you have revealed yourself in ages past,
and have blessed us with signs of your grace.

We praise you that through the waters of the sea,
you led your people Israel out of bondage,
into freedom in the land of your promise.

We praise you for sending Jesus your Son,
who for us was baptized in the waters of the Jordan,
and was anointed as the Christ by your Holy Spirit.
Through the baptism of his death and resurrection,
you set us free from the bondage of sin and death,
and give us cleansing and rebirth.

We praise you that in baptism
you give us your Holy Spirit,
who teaches us and leads us into all truth,
filling us with a variety of gifts,
that we might proclaim the gospel to all nations
and serve you as a royal priesthood.

Pour out your Spirit upon us and upon this water,
that this font may be your womb of new birth.
May *all* who now *pass* through these waters
be delivered from death to life,
from bondage to freedom,
from sin to righteousness.
Bind *them* to the household of faith,
guard *them* from all evil.
Strengthen *them* to serve you with joy
until the day you make all things new.
To you be all praise, honor, and glory;
through Jesus Christ our Savior,
who, with you and the Holy Spirit,
lives and reigns forever.
Amen.

D
Blessed are you, O God, maker and ruler of all things.
Your voice thundered over the waters at creation.
You water the mountains
and send springs into the valleys
to refresh and satisfy all living things.

Through the waters of the flood
you carried those in the ark to safety.
Through the sea you led your people Israel
from slavery to freedom.
In the wilderness you nourished them with water from the rock,
and you brought them across the river Jordan to the promised land.

By the baptism of his death and resurrection,
your Son Jesus has carried us to safety and freedom.
The floods shall not overwhelm us,
and the deep shall not swallow us up,
for Christ has brought us over to the land of promise.
He sends us to make disciples,
baptizing in the name of the Father, and of the Son, and of the Holy Spirit.

Pour out your Holy Spirit;
wash away sin in this cleansing water;
clothe the baptized with Christ;
and claim your daughters and sons,
no longer slave or free,
no longer male or female,
but one with all the baptized in Christ Jesus,
who lives and reigns with you
in the unity of the Holy Spirit,
one God, now and forever.
Amen.

E

Holy God, holy and merciful, holy and mighty,
you are the river of life,
you are the everlasting wellspring,
you are the fire of rebirth.

Glory to you for oceans and lakes, for rivers and creeks.
Honor to you for cloud and rain, for dew and snow.
Your waters are below us, around us, above us:
our life is born in you.
You are the fountain of resurrection.

Praise to you for your saving waters:
Noah and the animals survive the flood,
Hagar discovers your well.
The Israelites escape through the sea,
and they drink from your gushing rock.
Naaman washes his leprosy away,
and the Samaritan woman will never be thirsty again.

At this font, holy God, we pray:
Breathe your Spirit into this water,
and into all who are gathered here this *night*.
Illumine our days.
Enliven our bones.
Dry our tears.
Wash away the sin within us,
and drown the evil around us.
Satisfy all our thirst with your eternal fountain,
and bring to birth the body of Christ,
who lives with you and the Holy Spirit,
one God, now and forever.
Amen.

F

Blessed are you, holy God.
You are the creator of the waters of the earth.
You are the river of life.

You led your people through the river Jordan
and called them to life in covenant.
Your Son was baptized in the river Jordan
to begin his mission among us.

Come also into this water
and into those who are here baptized.
Create us all anew
that we may serve this needy world;
for we trust in the name of Jesus, your Son,
who lives with you and the Holy Spirit,
one God, now and forever.
Amen.

G

Blessed are you, holy God.
You are the creator of the waters of the earth.
You are the fire of rebirth.

You poured out your Spirit on your people Israel.
You breathe life into our dry bones.
Your Son promised to send the Spirit to us
that the world may know your peace and truth.

Breathe also into this water
and into those who are here baptized.
Adopt us all as your children
that we may embody your Spirit in the world;
for we call on the name of your Son,
who lives with you and the Holy Spirit,
one God, now and forever.
Amen.

H

Blessed are you, holy God.
You are the creator of the waters of the earth.
You are the everlasting wellspring.

You gather your people from sea to sea.
You quench our thirst, and you comfort all who weep.
Your Son stands among us, Shepherd and Lamb,
to lead all the saints through death to life.

Send your Spirit to dwell in this water
and in those who are here baptized.
May this water be a sign of the end of all tears;
for we stand under the name above every name, Jesus your Son,
who lives with you and the Holy Spirit,
one God, now and forever.
Amen.

BAPTISM

B

The candidate is immersed into the water, or water is poured on the candidate's head, as the presiding minister says:
<u>Name</u> is baptized in the name of the Father,
The candidate is immersed, or water is poured on the candidate's head a second time:
and of the Son,
The candidate is immersed, or water is poured on the candidate's head a third time:
and of the Holy Spirit.
Amen.

Acclamation

C

Blessed be God, who chose you in Christ.
Live in love as Christ loved us.

D

Springs of water, bless the Lord.
Give God glory and praise forever.

PRESENTATION OF A CANDLE

B

Let your light so shine before others
that they may see your good works
and glorify your Father in heaven.

Notes on the Rite

GENERAL

The order for baptism normally concludes a period of preparation. For infants and young children the preparation may include prayers with parents prior to birth or adoption, prayers that anticipate baptism following the birth or adoption of a child, and preparatory sessions with parents and sponsors preceding the baptism that cover the significance of baptism, the Christian responsibilities of parents and sponsors, and guidance about the liturgy of baptism itself. For older children and adults, preparation for baptism will ordinarily include an extended period of faith formation and instruction (that is, a catechumenate), guided by catechists, sponsors, pastors, and other leaders in the Christian community.

The context for the liturgy of baptism is ordinarily the primary Sunday assembly of the congregation around word and table. Typically the baptismal liturgy follows the hymn of the day, in place of the creed. It may also follow the apostolic greeting in the gathering rite, in which case the creed is not used later in the service.

As space allows, others from the assembly, especially children, may gather near the baptismal group and ministers at the font. If the assembly is not able to gather around the font, they may be seated for the rite, standing if possible for the confession of faith and the welcome.

When multiple candidates for baptism are present, a modification to the structure of the rite may place the baptism, laying on of hands, signing, and giving of a garment for one person, before going on to the baptism, laying on of hands, signing, and giving of a garment for each additional person in turn.

PRESENTATION

In the case of candidates unable to answer for themselves, parents may join the sponsors in speaking the words of presentation. The questions addressed to parents may be addressed also to others who serve as guardians for children or for other candidates unable to answer for themselves.

THANKSGIVING

The visible and audible sign of water being poured into the font may precede or accompany the prayer of thanksgiving. The water that is poured may be added to water that is already present in the font or pool.

While the thanksgiving prayer in the rite may be used on any occasion of baptism, the alternate forms of thanksgiving provided in the supplemental texts may be particularly appropriate for baptismal festivals (alternate B, C, D, or E for the Easter Vigil; alternate B, C, or F for the Baptism of Our Lord; alternate C or G for the Day of Pentecost; and alternate D or H for All Saints Day).

WELCOME

If the baptismal group has not been in clear view of the assembly throughout this liturgy, participants may process to a location suitable for the purpose of welcoming at the conclusion of this rite.

INTERCESSORY PRAYERS

When baptism takes place after the sermon and hymn of the day, the intercessions follow the rite of baptism. These prayers include petitions for the newly baptized, their sponsors, and parents and families.

Formation in Faith

Related to Baptism

Shape of the Process

The church accompanies the celebration of baptism in the worshiping assembly with a process of forming people in the Christian faith. An age-old pattern for this formation that has recently found new life among the churches offers a kind of apprenticeship in the Christian faith for older youth and adults that leads to and accompanies baptism. These persons participate in catechesis and formation as they prepare for baptism within a Christian community that is actively involved in the process of welcoming newcomers and sharing the faith with them.

Formation in faith involves the whole person—body, mind, heart, and soul. Formation in the Christian faith takes place through worship, reflection on scripture, prayer, and ministry in daily life. Faith formation happens in different ways for each individual. It is a lifelong process both before and after baptism rather than a series of stages in faith development. The following pattern, however, is a useful way for congregations to guide people who are preparing for baptism and for full participation in the life of the Christian community.

As the process unfolds, the worshiping assembly celebrates milestones along the path of baptismal formation. These rites are indicated by italics in the following paragraphs and are presented in order following this description of the shape of the process.

INQUIRY

Inquiry is an open-ended period of time during which inquirers make an initial exploration into Christian faith and life. This period of inquiry is shaped by the needs of the inquirer as well as by parish leaders and the congregation. When, after an open-ended time of inquiry and in consultation with a pastor, sponsor, or other leader, a person decides to enter a more intensive period of exploration of the Christian faith (a catechumenate), he or she is welcomed by the congregation at a principal Sunday service that may be celebrated at any time during the church year. In the rite of *Welcome of Inquirers*, the individual declares the desire to enter the next period of formation in the faith, and the congregation declares its intention to support this person through prayer and witness.

CATECHUMENATE

The catechumenate is an open-ended period of time during which catechumens, assisted by catechists and sponsors, explore the Christian faith more deeply through the reading of scripture, prayer, worship, and ministry in daily life. This period of reflection and study may last from several months to years. Near the conclusion of the catechumenate, during a rite of *Enrollment of Candidates for Baptism*, catechumens publicly express their desire

---

The process of formation in faith using the pattern of the catechumenate is described at greater length in the three-volume set of books and video titled *Welcome to Christ*. See the list of resources at the end of this volume.

to be baptized. For persons who will be baptized at the Vigil of Easter, this enrollment normally occurs on the first Sunday in Lent. Enrollment may take place on the first Sunday in Advent for those to be baptized on the Baptism of Our Lord, or on the Sunday nearest Holy Cross Day for those to be baptized on All Saints Day.

BAPTISMAL PREPARATION

A period of final baptismal preparation precedes the celebration of baptism. For candidates who will be baptized at the Vigil of Easter, Lent provides a six-week period ideally suited as an intensive period of preparation for baptism. During the Lenten season, the gospel readings for the third, fourth, and fifth Sundays set forth strong baptismal images. On these Sundays, the candidates preparing for baptism are invited to receive God's blessing and the prayers of the congregation in rites of *Blessing of Candidates*. Alternatives are also given in these orders of worship for blessings that occur outside of Lent. This is also a time when presentations of the creed and the church's life of prayer may be made.

Baptism stands at the center of the catechumenal process. When baptism occurs at the Vigil of Easter, the relationship of baptism to the death and resurrection of Christ is reinforced. The proclamation of the history of salvation during the Vigil of Easter leads the community to the font where new brothers and sisters are born of water and the word, and the baptized affirm their baptismal promises. From the font, the entire community gathers at the table to celebrate the communion.

BAPTISMAL LIVING

The process of formation in faith does not end with baptism. Especially during the period of time immediately following baptism, the church leads the newly-baptized into the new life in Christ they have received in the sacraments. Easter ushers in the lifetime of baptismal living for those newly baptized at the Vigil of Easter. This period extends throughout the fifty days of Easter and beyond. A rite of *Affirmation of Christian Vocation* may be celebrated during which the newly baptized affirm their various callings ("vocations") in daily life. For those who were baptized at the Vigil of Easter, it is particularly appropriate to celebrate this affirmation of the day of Pentecost. Whenever the affirmation of vocation is observed, it is a fitting celebration for the newly baptized and an appropriate form of God's blessing on those who have entered fully into the life and witness of the congregation.

WELCOME of INQUIRERS

Outline

GATHERING
Before the entrance hymn or after the prayer of the day:
Presentation

WORD
After the hymn of the day:
Signing with the Cross
Presentation of the Bible
Blessing
The Prayers

MEAL

SENDING

WELCOME of INQUIRERS

This welcome of those inquiring into Christian faith and life may be used whenever there are people who desire to begin a more public relationship with a Christian congregation. This rite is intended to be used during the principal Sunday liturgy of the congregation.

PRESENTATION

At the door, before the entrance hymn, inquirers and their sponsors gather with the ministers to be welcomed to the catechumenate. The assembly faces them. The presentation may also take place following the prayer of the day, in which case the inquirers and their sponsors may be invited to stand at their places or to stand before the presiding minister.

The presiding minister addresses the assembly:
Dear friends, we are gathered [at this door] today
to meet *these persons* who have been called by God's Spirit
to inquire into the Christian faith
and life in this congregation.
Together, let us welcome *them* to this community of faith in Jesus Christ.

A sponsor presents each inquirer:
I present <u>name</u> to be welcomed by this congregation.

With these or similar words, the presiding minister asks each person presented:
What do you ask of God's church?
Response: To hear God's word with you.

What do you seek from God's word?
Response: Faith and fullness of life.

The presiding minister continues:
Grace and mercy are given to all who call upon God's name.
We pray that God may lead you to Christ in baptism.
Now I invite you to join with this assembly to hear the word of God.
Will you be faithful in learning the way of Christ?
Each inquirer responds: I will, and I ask God to help me.

The presiding minister addresses the sponsors and the assembly:
Sponsors, you now present *these inquirers* to us.
All of you who are assembled here are called to welcome and support
these inquirers and *their sponsors*.
Will you help *them* hear the gospel of Christ and come into the household of faith?
We will, and we ask God to help us.

The presiding minister continues:
Let us pray.
Merciful God,
we give you thanks for *name/s*
whom you have sought and summoned in many ways.
You have called *them* today and *they* have answered you in our presence.
We praise you, O God, and we bless you.
We praise you, O God, and we bless you.

The assisting minister addresses the inquirers:
Now, *name/s*, come [into the church] and hear the word of God with us.

The liturgy continues with the entrance hymn. The inquirers and their sponsors may join the entrance procession and take their places in the assembly together.

SIGNING WITH THE CROSS

Following the hymn of the day, the inquirers and their sponsors gather before the assembly.

The presiding minister addresses the inquirers with these or similar words:
You have heard the holy and saving gospel of our Lord Jesus Christ.
Now receive the sign of that gospel on your body and in your heart,
that you may know the Lord and the power of his resurrection.

A sponsor traces a cross on the inquirer's forehead as the presiding minister says:
Receive the ✝ cross on your forehead,
a sign of God's endless love and mercy for you.
Learn to know and to follow Christ.

One of the following or another response may be sung or spoken by the assembly:

A

**Praise to you, O Christ,
the wisdom and power of God.**

B

**Glory and praise to you,
almighty and gracious God.**

The presiding minister may continue. A sponsor or catechist may trace a cross on each part of the inquirer's body as it is named.

Receive the ✝ cross on your ears,
that you may hear the gospel of Christ, the word of life. *Response*

Receive the ✝ cross on your eyes,
that you may see the light of Christ, illumination for your way *Response*

Receive the ✝ cross on your lips,
that you may sing the praise of Christ, the joy of the church. *Response*

Receive the ✝ cross on your heart,
that God may dwell there by faith. *Response*

Receive the ✝ cross on your shoulders,
that you may bear the gentle yoke of Christ. *Response*

Receive the ✝ cross on your hands,
that God's mercy may be known in your work. *Response*

Receive the ✝ cross on your feet,
that you may walk in the way of Christ. *Response*

PRESENTATION OF THE BIBLE

A representative of the congregation presents a Bible to each inquirer with these or similar words:
Receive this Bible.
Hear God's word with us.
Learn and tell its stories.
Discover its mysteries.
Honor its commandments.
Rejoice in its good news.
May God's life-giving word, sweeter than honey,
inspire you and make you wise.

BLESSING

*The inquirers may kneel. The presiding minister may extend both hands over the inquirers or may
lay a hand on each inquirer's head during the prayer:*
Let us pray.
Merciful and most high God,
creator and life-giver of all that is,
you have called all people
from darkness into light,
from error into truth,
from death into life.
We ask you:
Grant grace to *name/s* and bless *them*.
Raise *them* by your Spirit.
Revive *them* by your word.
Form *them* by your hand.
Bring *them* to the water of life
and to the bread and cup of blessing,
that with all your people
they may bear witness to your grace
and praise you forever
through Jesus Christ our Lord.
Amen.

The assisting minister addresses the inquirers with these or similar words:
God bring you in peace and joy to fullness of life in Christ
and call you to the waters of baptism.
Amen.

The inquirers and their sponsors return to their places. One of the following or another response may be sung or spoken by the assembly:

A

**May the God of all grace
who has called you to glory
support you and make you strong.**

B

**Blessed be God who chose you in Christ.
Live in love as Christ loved us.**

The liturgy continues with the intercessory prayers, which include petitions for the inquirers (who now may be named catechumens) and for all who participate in the congregation's ministry of formation.

ENROLLMENT of CANDIDATES for BAPTISM

Outline

GATHERING

WORD
After the hymn of the day:
Presentation
Enrollment of Names
Blessing
The Prayers

MEAL

SENDING

ENROLLMENT of CANDIDATES for BAPTISM

When candidates are preparing for baptism at the Vigil of Easter, enrollment normally takes place during the principal service of the congregation on the first Sunday in Lent. When baptism takes place at another time during the church year, enrollment normally precedes baptism by a comparable period of time.

If the names of candidates for baptism are to be written in a book as part of the rite, a large and beautiful book lies open at a place in the midst of the congregation where it can be easily seen and used. This book may be placed near the list of those for whom the congregation prays each time it gathers.

PRESENTATION

Following the hymn of the day, the candidates, sponsors, and catechists gather before the assembly near the place where the book of names is located.

The catechist presents the candidates with these or similar words:
The following *persons* desire to make public *their* intention to be baptized
[at the coming festival of our Lord's death and resurrection].

The presiding minister asks the candidates:
By God's grace you have been drawn to this congregation.
You have heard the word of God and prayed with us.
Do you desire to be baptized?
Each candidate responds: I do.

The presiding minister addresses the sponsors with these or similar words:
You have been companions to *these women and men* in *their* journey of faith.
Have *they* been faithful in hearing the word of God
and in receiving it as the pattern for *their* lives?
Response: Yes, by the grace of God.

The minister addresses the assembly with these or similar words:
People of God, [as you journey through Lent,]
will you support *these candidates*, chosen by God,
through your prayer, presence, and example?
[As you observe the disciplines of Lent,]
will you be for *them* a community of love and growth in God's grace?
We will, and we ask God to help us.

A representative of the congregation presents the candidates:
The following *persons are candidates* for baptism: *name/s*.
We welcome you to this time of preparation for baptism.

ENROLLMENT OF NAMES

A sponsor or catechist may write the name of each person to be baptized in the congregation's book, or the candidate may sign his or her own name in the book while a catechist reads out each name for the congregation to hear.

After each name is read aloud, and while the names are inscribed in the book, one of the following or another response may be sung:

A

**God calls you to be one
with Jesus Christ our Lord.**

B

**Lord Jesus, you call your own by name,
and lead them to waters of life.**

BLESSING

The candidates may kneel. The presiding minister may extend both hands over the candidates or may lay a hand on each candidate's head during the prayer:

Let us pray.
Merciful and most high God,
creator and life-giver of all that is,
you have called all people
from darkness into light,
from error into truth,
from death into life.
We ask you:
Grant grace to *name/s* and bless *them.*
Raise *them* by your Spirit.
Revive *them* by your word.
Form *them* by your hand.
Bring *them* to the water of life
and to the bread and cup of blessing,
that with all your people
they may bear witness to your grace
and praise you forever
through Jesus Christ our Lord.
Amen.

The assisting minister addresses the candidates with these or similar words:
[Journey with us now through Lent
as we prepare for the festival of our Lord's death and resurrection.]
God bring you in peace and joy to the day of your baptism
and to fullness of life in Christ.
Amen.

The candidates and sponsors return to their places. One of the following or another response may be sung or spoken by the assembly:

A	B
May the God of all grace who has called you to glory support you and make you strong.	**Blessed be God who chose you in Christ. Live in love as Christ loved us.**

The liturgy continues with the intercessory prayers, which include petitions for the candidates and for all those preparing for baptism.

BLESSING of CANDIDATES
Confession of Faith

Outline

GATHERING

WORD
After the hymn of the day:
Invitation
Presentation of the Creed
Testimony of Faith
Blessing
The Prayers

MEAL

SENDING

BLESSING of CANDIDATES
Confession of Faith

The blessing of candidates is intended to keep the candidates for baptism in the prayers of the congregation during the final weeks of their preparation. This blessing may be used on the third Sunday in Lent when candidates are preparing for baptism at the Vigil of Easter, or on a Sunday several weeks before baptism at another time in the church year.

INVITATION

Following the hymn of the day, the candidates and their sponsors gather at the font.
The presiding minister addresses the candidates with these or similar words:

Third Sunday in Lent, year A

As the woman of Samaria confessed her faith in Jesus Christ,
the giver of the water of life,
so the church confesses its need of Christ and its trust in God's mercy.
We invite you whom God has chosen for baptism
to join all the people of God in confessing the faith of the church.

Third Sunday in Lent, year B

As the temple of God revealed its need for cleansing
when Jesus went up to Jerusalem,
so the church confesses its need of Christ and its trust in God's mercy.
We invite you whom God has chosen for baptism
to join all the people of God in confessing the faith of the church.

Third Sunday in Lent, year C

As the barren fig tree required the gardener's care
in order to thrive and bear fruit,
so the church confesses its need of Christ and its trust in God's mercy.
We invite you whom God has chosen for baptism
to join all the people of God in confessing the faith of the church.

At other times

As the people of Israel praised God for delivering them from slavery
and bringing them to the promised land,
so the church confesses its need of Christ and its trust in God's mercy.
We invite you whom God has chosen for baptism
to join all the people of God in confessing the faith of the church.

PRESENTATION OF THE CREED

The assembly responds with the creed, confessing it before and with the candidates:

I believe in God, the Father almighty,
   creator of heaven and earth.

I believe in Jesus Christ, God's only Son, our Lord,
   who was conceived by the Holy Spirit,
   born of the virgin Mary,
   suffered under Pontius Pilate,
   was crucified, died, and was buried;
   he descended to the dead.
   On the third day he rose again;
   he ascended into heaven,
   he is seated at the right hand of the Father,
   and he will come to judge the living and the dead.

I believe in the Holy Spirit,
   the holy catholic church,
   the communion of saints,
   the forgiveness of sins,
   the resurrection of the body,
   and the life everlasting. Amen.

A copy of the creed may be presented to each candidate. Bishops may provide such copies as a sign of the participation of the wider church in the candidates' preparation.

A catechism may also be presented to each candidate.

TESTIMONY OF FAITH

Following the creed, the presiding minister may invite the candidates to offer a testimony of faith.

BLESSING

The candidates may kneel. The presiding minister may extend both hands over the candidates or may lay a hand on each candidate's head during the prayer:
Let us pray.
Merciful and most high God,
creator and life-giver of all that is,
you have called all people
from darkness into light,
from error into truth,
from death into life.
We ask you:
Grant grace to *name/s* and bless *them*.
Raise *them* by your Spirit.
Revive *them* by your word.
Form *them* by your hand.
Bring *them* to the water of life
and to the bread and cup of blessing,
that with all your people
they may bear witness to your grace
and praise you forever
through Jesus Christ our Lord.
Amen.

The assisting minister addresses the candidates with these or similar words:
God bring you in peace and joy to the day of your baptism
and to fullness of life in Christ.
Amen.

The candidates and sponsors return to their places. One of the following or another response may be sung or spoken by the assembly:

A

May the God of all grace
who has called you to glory
support you and make you strong.

B

Blessed be God who chose you in Christ.
Live in love as Christ loved us.

The liturgy continues with the intercessory prayers, which include petitions for the candidates and for all those preparing for baptism.

Notes on the Rite

These blessings carry on the tradition of the Lenten "scrutiny" (examination) of candidates for baptism, combining that tradition with the practice of handing over to the candidates both the church's creed and the Christian pattern of prayer.

These rites are ordinarily intended for adult candidates who have not yet been baptized. However, those persons who are preparing for affirmation of baptism may also be included in the group that comes forward.

If the group of candidates includes those who are preparing for affirmation of baptism, the presiding minister may change the invitation as follows:
>We invite you whom God has chosen for baptism
>and those preparing for the affirmation of baptism
>to join all the people of God in confessing the faith of the church.

Beautifully lettered or printed copies of the creed may be presented to the candidates. Bishops may choose to provide such copies and a letter of welcome as a mark of the participation of the wider church in the candidates' preparation.

When a catechism is presented, an assisting minister may give it with these or similar words:
>Receive this summary of the faith of the church.
>Learn it. Pray it. Take it to heart.
>Join us in studying it.

Candidates must be carefully prepared for the testimony of faith in their study groups. Candidates should be advised to speak briefly and simply.

If the group of candidates includes those who are preparing for affirmation of baptism, the assisting minister may change the words of the dismissal as follows:
>God bring you in peace and joy to the day of your baptism and baptismal renewal
>and to fullness of life in Christ.

BLESSING of CANDIDATES
Renunciation of Evil

Outline

GATHERING

WORD
  After the hymn of the day:
Renunciation of Evil
Blessing
The Prayers

MEAL

SENDING

BLESSING of CANDIDATES
Renunciation of Evil

The blessing of candidates is intended to keep the candidates for baptism in the prayers of the congregation during the final weeks of their preparation. This blessing may be used on the fourth Sunday in Lent when candidates are preparing for baptism at the Vigil of Easter, or on a Sunday several weeks before baptism at another time in the church year.

RENUNCIATION OF EVIL

Following the hymn of the day, the candidates and their sponsors gather at the font.
The presiding minister addresses the assembly with these or similar words:

Fourth Sunday in Lent, year A
As the man born blind received his sight and witnessed boldly to the light of Christ,
so the church, empowered by the Spirit, renounces the power of evil in the world.
Let us join with saints and angels to pray that God will expose the devil's empty promises
and flood the world with light.

Fourth Sunday in Lent, year B
As Jesus calls us to turn away from darkness and to live in the light of God,
so the church, empowered by the Spirit, renounces the power of evil in the world.
Let us join with saints and angels to pray that God will expose the devil's empty promises
and flood the world with light.

Fourth Sunday in Lent, year C
As the prodigal son abandoned his life of sin and returned to the joy of the father,
so the church, empowered by the Spirit, renounces the power of evil in the world.
Let us join with saints and angels to pray that God will expose the devil's empty promises
and flood the world with light.

At other times
As the prophets called for God's people to reject sin and to live in God's covenant of love,
so the church, empowered by the Spirit, renounces the power of evil in the world.
Let us join with saints and angels to pray that God will expose the devil's empty promises
and flood the world with light.

The presiding minister continues with these or similar words:
Let us pray.
Lord God, you promised that the ancient evil of the serpent
would be vanquished on the cross of your Son.
We ask you: Crush the power of the devil.
Protect your people from the evils of the world.
Preserve us from sin and error,
that with saints and angels we may live in the joy of your goodness and truth,
through Jesus Christ our Lord.
Amen.

BLESSING

The candidates may kneel. The presiding minister may extend both hands over the candidates or may lay a hand on each candidate's head during the prayer:
Let us pray.
Merciful and most high God, creator and life-giver of all that is,
you have called all people from darkness into light,
from error into truth, from death into life.
We ask you: Grant grace to *name/s* and bless *them*.
Raise *them* by your Spirit.
Revive *them* by your word.
Form *them* by your hand.
Bring *them* to the water of life and to the bread and cup of blessing,
that with all your people *they* may bear witness to your grace
and praise you forever through Jesus Christ our Lord.
Amen.

The assisting minister addresses the candidates with these or similar words:
God bring you in peace and joy to the day of your baptism
and to fullness of life in Christ.
Amen.

The candidates and sponsors return to their places. One of the following or another response may be sung or spoken by the assembly:

A

**May the God of all grace
who has called you to glory
support you and make you strong.**

B

**Blessed be God who chose you in Christ.
Live in love as Christ loved us.**

The liturgy continues with the intercessory prayers, which include petitions for the candidates and for all those preparing for baptism.

Notes on the Rite

These blessings carry on the tradition of the Lenten "scrutiny" (examination) of candidates for baptism, combining that tradition with the practice of handing over to the candidates both the church's creed and the Christian pattern of prayer.

These rites are ordinarily intended for adult candidates who have not yet been baptized. However, those persons who are preparing for affirmation of baptism may also be included in the group that comes forward.

If the group of candidates includes those who are preparing for affirmation of baptism, the assisting minister may change the words of the dismissal as follows:

God bring you in peace and joy to the day of your baptism and baptismal renewal and to fullness of life in Christ.

BLESSING of CANDIDATES
Commitment to Prayer

Outline

GATHERING

WORD
  After the creed:
Commitment to Prayer
The Prayers
Presentation of a Book of Worship
Blessing

MEAL

SENDING

BLESSING of CANDIDATES
Commitment to Prayer

The blessing of candidates is intended to keep the candidates for baptism in the prayers of the congregation during the final weeks of their preparation. This blessing may be used on the fifth Sunday in Lent when candidates are preparing for baptism at the Vigil of Easter, or on a Sunday several weeks before baptism at another time in the church year.

COMMITMENT TO PRAYER

Following the creed, the candidates and their sponsors gather at the font.
The presiding minister addresses the candidates with these or similar words:

Fifth Sunday in Lent, year A
As Mary and Martha prayed for their brother Lazarus,
so the church prays for you and for all the needs of the world,
confident in the life-giving presence and mercy of Christ.

Fifth Sunday in Lent, year B
As the disciples were taught to follow Jesus by living their life for others,
so the church prays for you and for all the needs of the world,
confident in the life-giving presence and mercy of Christ.

Fifth Sunday in Lent, year C
As Mary of Bethany honored Jesus with her love and concern,
so the church prays for you and for all the needs of the world,
confident in the life-giving presence and mercy of Christ.

At other times
As the disciples were taught by Jesus to pray for the coming of God's reign,
so the church prays for you and for all the needs of the world,
confident in the life-giving presence and mercy of Christ.

THE PRAYERS

The candidates and their sponsors remain standing at the front of the assembly while the assisting minister leads the prayers. During the petitions for those preparing for baptism, the sponsors may place a hand on the shoulder of each candidate.

PRESENTATION OF A BOOK OF WORSHIP

A representative of the congregation may present a book of worship to each candidate with these or similar words:
Receive this book of worship.
We ask you to join us in prayer and song to God.

BLESSING

The candidates may kneel. The presiding minister may extend both hands over the candidates or may lay a hand on each candidate's head during the prayer:
Let us pray.
Merciful and most high God,
creator and life-giver of all that is,
you have called all people
from darkness into light,
from error into truth,
from death into life.
We ask you:
Grant grace to *name/s* and bless *them*.
Raise *them* by your Spirit.
Revive *them* by your word.
Form *them* by your hand.
Bring *them* to the water of life
and to the bread and cup of blessing,
that with all your people
they may bear witness to your grace
and praise you forever
through Jesus Christ our Lord.
Amen.

The assisting minister addresses the candidates with these or similar words:
God bring you in peace and joy to the day of your baptism
and to fullness of life in Christ.
Amen.

The candidates and sponsors return to their places. The assembly may sing one of the following or another response:

A	B
May the God of all grace who has called you to glory support you and make you strong.	**Blessed be God who chose you in Christ. Live in love as Christ loved us.**

The liturgy continues with the greeting of peace.

Notes on the Rite

These blessings carry on the tradition of the Lenten "scrutiny" (examination) of candidates for baptism, combining that tradition with the practice of handing over to the candidates both the church's creed and the Christian pattern of prayer.

These rites are ordinarily intended for adult candidates who have not yet been baptized. However, those persons who are preparing for affirmation of baptism may also be included in the group that comes forward.

Honoring ecumenical practice, the congregation may "present" the Lord's Prayer to the candidates for baptism by singing or saying it at the conclusion of the intercessory prayers. The candidates have already "received" it in written form (if the catechism was presented earlier in the process). If the Lord's Prayer is used here, it is also used in the great thanksgiving in the liturgy of the eucharist.

This presentation of the church's worship book is intended to symbolize the inclusion of the candidates in the prayer life not only of the local assembly but of the Lutheran church. A book that includes those elements named in the catechism and customarily used in worship (the Apostles' Creed, liturgies of baptism and eucharist, confession and forgiveness, daily prayer) is most appropriate. This is not the presentation of a book of songs but the core resources for worship of a Lutheran community, to which the candidate can turn. If a worship book has already been given, the presentation may be omitted here.

If the group of candidates includes those who are preparing for affirmation of baptism, the assisting minister may change the words of the dismissal as follows:
> God bring you in peace and joy to the day of your baptism and baptismal renewal
> and to fullness of life in Christ.

AFFIRMATION of CHRISTIAN VOCATION

Outline

GATHERING

WORD

MEAL

SENDING
Affirmation of Vocation
Blessing
Dismissal

AFFIRMATION of CHRISTIAN VOCATION

In preparation for this rite, it is important that those affirming Christian vocation be given adequate time to reflect on their place in the body of Christ and the vocation that they wish to affirm. Such preparation would certainly include reflection on how God's gifts of baptism, absolution, and communion shape the life of the Christian in the world.

The description of the area of service need not be extensive. The pastor and/or catechist may wish to assist in preparing this description. This is also a suitable project for discussion in the small groups with the catechist following baptism.

When set within the liturgy of holy communion, this order is used to conclude the sending rite. The service may be adapted to other liturgical settings or other places within the liturgy.

AFFIRMATION OF VOCATION

Those affirming Christian vocation together with their sponsors gather with the ministers at the baptismal font. They may carry their baptismal candles. These candles are then lighted from the paschal candle by an assisting minister.

The presiding minister addresses the assembly with these or similar words:
Dear Christian friends:
Baptized into the priesthood of Christ,
we are all called by the Holy Spirit
to offer ourselves to the Lord of all creation
in thanksgiving for all that God has done and continues to do for us.
It is our privilege to affirm those who are endeavoring
to carry out their vocation as Christians in the world.

A representative of the congregation says:
Through holy baptism God has set us free from sin
and made us members of the priesthood we share in Christ Jesus.
Through word and sacrament we have been nurtured in faith,
that we may give praise to God
and bear God's creative and redeeming word to all the world.

A sponsor presents each newly baptized person and gives a brief description of the area of service to be affirmed. Each person presented may briefly comment on the significance of this choice.

The congregation may sing one of the following or another response after each person's comments:

A	B
May the God of all grace	**Blessed be God who chose you in Christ.**
who has called you to glory	**Live in love as Christ loved us.**
support you and make you strong.	

The presiding minister addresses those affirming Christian vocation:
Name/s, both your work and your rest are in God.
Will you endeavor to pattern your life on the Lord Jesus Christ,
in gratitude to God and in service to others,
at morning and evening, at work and at play,
all the days of your life?
Response: I will, and I ask God to help me.

Let us pray.
Almighty God,
by the power of the Spirit you have knit these your servants
into the one body of your Son, Jesus Christ.
Look with favor upon them in their commitment to serve in Christ's name.
Give them courage, patience, and vision;
and strengthen us all in our Christian vocation
of witness to the world and of service to others;
through Jesus Christ our Lord.
Amen.

BLESSING

The assisting minister addresses the assembly with these or similar words:
Go out into the world in peace;
be of good courage;
hold to what is good;
return no one evil for evil;
strengthen the faint-hearted;
support the weak;
help the suffering;
honor all people;
love and serve our God,
rejoicing in the power of the Holy Spirit.

The presiding minister blesses the assembly:
The almighty and merciful God, Father, ✛ Son, and Holy Spirit,
bless you now and forever.
Amen.

DISMISSAL

The assisting minister may dismiss the assembly:
Go in peace. Serve the Lord.
Thanks be to God.

Affirmation
of Baptism

Shape of the Rite

Although a person is baptized once in a lifetime, the gifts of holy baptism are continually renewed in the lives of God's people. In addition to a daily return to baptism in remembrance and thanksgiving, Affirmation of Baptism is a rite that may be used to mark significant milestones in the journey of the individual believer or the community of faith. Those who have been baptized at one time in their life may affirm their baptism as a sign of their renewed participation in the life of the church, or at the outset of their association with a particular congregation. Those who have been baptized at an early age often come through a period of nurture in the church to an affirmation of their baptism in young adulthood. Affirmation of Baptism may also be used to mark significant life passages, times of growth in faith, and as a public rite of renewal by a congregation at particular times and seasons.

PRESENTATION
Introduction
Presentation
Prayer

During the principal liturgy of the congregation, at the conclusion of the hymn of the day, the ministers come to the font to lead the rite of affirmation. When the rite of affirmation includes individual persons who are affirming their baptism in the presence of the assembly, they also gather at the font, and may be accompanied by sponsors and others from the assembly, such as parents, catechists, and mentors. The presiding minister may note briefly the occasion for this affirmation. Individual affirmers are then presented to the congregation by name, and prayer may be offered for them.

PROFESSION
Renunciation of Evil
Profession of Faith
Commitment

Affirmation of baptism includes a public profession of faith, as the baptized echo the words of renunciation of evil and confession of faith that were first spoken at their baptism. Through questions and responses that further unfold the meaning of baptism, those affirming baptism commit themselves to continuing in the covenant of baptism with the help of God.

BLESSING
Prayer of Blessing
Laying On of Hands

The presiding minister prays for the blessing of God upon those who are affirming their baptism, echoing the prayer for the Holy Spirit at baptism and asking for a strengthening of the spiritual gifts bestowed in baptism. The presiding minister may lay hands upon the head of individual affirmers to accompany the blessing, and others who surround them may add a blessing.

ACCLAMATION
Acclamation
Baptismal Remembrance

In response to the affirmation of baptism, the assembly praises God and offers acclamation to the promises and blessings that have been spoken. Thanksgiving by the whole assembly for the gift of baptism may be expressed in prayer, song, and symbolic action, using the tangible elements associated with baptism (such as water or the oil of anointing) in a way that is clearly a reminder rather than an enactment of baptism. The intercessory prayers that follow include all who affirm their baptism.

AFFIRMATION of BAPTISM

Outline

PRESENTATION
Introduction
Presentation
Prayer

PROFESSION
Renunciation of Evil
Profession of Faith
Commitment

BLESSING
Prayer of Blessing
Laying On of Hands

ACCLAMATION
Acclamation
Baptismal Remembrance

AFFIRMATION of BAPTISM
Public Profession of Faith

This rite is intended for use with baptized Christians who desire to affirm their baptism in the presence of the assembly. These persons include those who have been baptized at one time in their life and now desire to affirm their baptism in a variety of circumstances: as part of a process of formation in faith in youth or adulthood, at the time of beginning their participation in a new community of faith, as a sign of renewed participation in the life of the church, or at the time of a significant life passage.

Within the Sunday liturgy, at the conclusion of the hymn of the day, those who are affirming baptism may gather with the ministers at the font. They may be joined by others from the assembly.

PRESENTATION

INTRODUCTION

The presiding minister may address the assembly in these or similar words:
Dear friends, we give thanks to God for the gift of baptism
and for *these persons*, one with us in the body of Christ,
who *affirm their* baptism this day.
The presiding minister may note briefly the occasion for this affirmation.

PRESENTATION

Those affirming baptism are presented by a sponsor or another representative of the congregation:
I present *name/s,* who *desire* to affirm *their* baptism.

PRAYER

The presiding minister may pray in these or similar words:
Let us pray.
Merciful God, we thank you for *name/s,*
whom you have made your own by water and the word in baptism.
You have called *them* to yourself,
enlightened *them* with the gifts of your Spirit,
and nourished *them* in the community of faith.
Uphold your *servants* as *they affirm* the gifts and promises of baptism,
and unite the hearts of all whom you have brought to new birth
through this holy sacrament.
We ask this in the name of Christ.
Amen.

PROFESSION

RENUNCIATION OF EVIL

The presiding minister addresses those affirming baptism:
As you affirm your baptism,
I ask you to reject sin, profess your faith in Christ, and confess the faith of the church.

Do you renounce the devil
    and all the forces that defy God?
Response: I renounce them.

Do you renounce the powers of this world
    that rebel against God?
Response: I renounce them.

Do you renounce the ways of sin
    that draw you from God?
Response: I renounce them.

PROFESSION OF FAITH

The presiding minister may also say to those affirming baptism:
Do you turn to Christ as your Lord and Savior?
Response: In faith I turn to Christ.

The presiding minister addresses the assembly:
With the whole church, let us confess our faith.

Do you believe in God the Father?
I believe in God, the Father almighty,
    creator of heaven and earth.

Do you believe in Jesus Christ, the Son of God?
I believe in Jesus Christ, God's only Son, our Lord,
    who was conceived by the Holy Spirit,
    born of the virgin Mary,
    suffered under Pontius Pilate,
    was crucified, died, and was buried;
    he descended to the dead.
On the third day he rose again;
    he ascended into heaven,
    he is seated at the right hand of the Father,
    and he will come to judge the living and the dead.

Do you believe in God the Holy Spirit?
I believe in the Holy Spirit,
> **the holy catholic church,**
> **the communion of saints,**
> **the forgiveness of sins,**
> **the resurrection of the body,**
> **and the life everlasting. Amen.**

COMMITMENT

The presiding minister addresses those making affirmation:
You have made public profession of your faith.
Do you intend to continue in the covenant God made with you in holy baptism:
> to live among God's faithful people,
> to hear the word of God and share in the Lord's supper,
> to proclaim the good news of God in Christ through word and deed,
> to serve all people, following the example of Jesus,
> and to strive for justice and peace in all the earth?

Each affirmer responds: I do, and I ask God to help and guide me.

The presiding minister addresses the assembly:
People of God, do you promise to support *these sisters and brothers*
and pray for *them* in *their* life in Christ?
We do, and we ask God to help and guide us.

BLESSING

PRAYER OF BLESSING

Those affirming baptism may kneel. The presiding minister continues:
Let us pray.
We give you thanks, O God,
that through water and the Holy Spirit
you give us new birth, wash us from sin,
and raise us to eternal life.
The following blessing may be repeated for each affirmer. The presiding minister may lay both hands on the head of each person while speaking the blessing:
Stir up in <u>name</u> the gift of your Holy Spirit:
the spirit of wisdom and understanding,
the spirit of counsel and might,
the spirit of knowledge and the fear of the Lord,
the spirit of joy in your presence,
both now and forever.
Amen.

Sponsors or other representatives of the congregation may offer additional blessings.

ACCLAMATION

ACCLAMATION

The ministers and the affirmers face the assembly. A representative of the congregation addresses the assembly in these or similar words:
Let us give thanks for *those* affirming baptism
as we carry out the life of this Christian community
and its mission in the world.

The assembly addresses those affirming baptism:
As your sisters and brothers in the body of Christ,
we rejoice with you as you affirm your baptism.
Together let us give praise to God
and bear God's creative and redeeming word
to all the world.

BAPTISMAL REMEMBRANCE

This baptismal remembrance may be used to conclude the rite.

The presiding minister addresses the assembly in these or similar words:
When we were joined to Christ in the waters of baptism,
we were clothed with God's mercy and forgiveness.
Together let us remember our baptism.

The presiding minister gives thanks:
Blessed are you, O God of grace.
From age to age you made water a sign of your presence among us.
In the beginning your Spirit brooded over the waters
and you created the world by your word,
calling forth life in which you took delight.
You led Israel safely through the Red Sea into the land of promise,
and in the waters of the Jordan, you proclaimed Jesus your beloved one.
By water and the Spirit you adopted us as your daughters and sons,
making us heirs of the promise and servants of God.
Through this water remind us of our baptism.
Shower us with your Spirit,
that your forgiveness, grace, and love may be renewed in our lives.
To you be given honor and praise through Jesus Christ our Lord
in the unity of the Holy Spirit, now and forever.
Amen.

The acclamation may continue with a hymn, song, or psalm, during which the assembly may remember their baptism through a symbolic gesture: water from the font may be sprinkled upon the assembly, worshipers may touch the water and trace a sign of the cross upon themselves, or another appropriate action may be used.

At the conclusion of this action, the presiding minister addresses the assembly:
Almighty God,
who has given us a new birth by water and the Holy Spirit,
and bestowed on us the forgiveness of sins,
keep us in eternal life
through the grace of Jesus Christ our Lord.
Amen.

The liturgy continues with the intercessory prayers. Those affirming their baptism are included in the petitions.

AFFIRMATION of BAPTISM
Confirmation

In addition to Affirmation of Baptism: Public Profession of Faith, this rite may also be used with young adults who desire to affirm their baptism in the presence of the assembly to mark a significant milestone in their lifelong journey of nurture and formation in faith.

Within the Sunday liturgy, at the conclusion of the hymn of the day, those who are affirming baptism may gather with the ministers at the font. They may be joined by parents, sponsors, mentors, or others from the assembly.

PRESENTATION

INTRODUCTION

The presiding minister addresses the assembly in these or similar words:
Dear friends, we give thanks to God for the gift of baptism
and for *these persons,* one with us in the body of Christ,
who *affirm their* baptism this day
as a sign of *their* participation in the life of this community of faith
and its mission in the world.

PRESENTATION

Those affirming baptism are presented by a sponsor or another representative of the congregation:
I present *name/s,* who *desire* to affirm *their* baptism.

PRAYER

The presiding minister may pray in these or similar words:
Let us pray.
Merciful God, we thank you for *name/s,*
whom you have made your own by water and the word in baptism.
You have called *them* to yourself,
enlightened *them* with the gifts of your Spirit,
and nourished *them* in the community of faith.
Uphold your *servants* as *they affirm* the gifts and promises of baptism,
and unite the hearts of all whom you have brought to new birth
through this holy sacrament.
We ask this in the name of Christ.
Amen.

PROFESSION

RENUNCIATION OF EVIL

The presiding minister addresses those affirming baptism:
As you affirm your baptism,
I ask you to reject sin, profess your faith in Christ, and confess the faith of the church.

Do you renounce the devil
    and all the forces that defy God?
Response: I renounce them.

Do you renounce the powers of this world
    that rebel against God?
Response: I renounce them.

Do you renounce the ways of sin
    that draw you from God?
Response: I renounce them.

PROFESSION OF FAITH

The presiding minister may also say to those affirming baptism:
Do you turn to Christ as your Lord and Savior?
Response: In faith I turn to Christ.

The presiding minister addresses the assembly:
With the whole church, let us confess our faith.

Do you believe in God the Father?
**I believe in God, the Father almighty,
    creator of heaven and earth.**

Do you believe in Jesus Christ, the Son of God?
**I believe in Jesus Christ, God's only Son, our Lord,
    who was conceived by the Holy Spirit,
    born of the virgin Mary,
    suffered under Pontius Pilate,
    was crucified, died, and was buried;
    he descended to the dead.
On the third day he rose again;
    he ascended into heaven,
    he is seated at the right hand of the Father,
    and he will come to judge the living and the dead.**

Do you believe in God the Holy Spirit?
I believe in the Holy Spirit,
 the holy catholic church,
 the communion of saints,
 the forgiveness of sins,
 the resurrection of the body,
 and the life everlasting. Amen.

COMMITMENT

The presiding minister addresses those making affirmation:
You have made public profession of your faith.
Do you intend to continue in the covenant God made with you in holy baptism:
 to live among God's faithful people,
 to hear the word of God and share in the Lord's supper,
 to proclaim the good news of God in Christ through word and deed,
 to serve all people, following the example of Jesus,
 and to strive for justice and peace in all the earth?
Each affirmer responds: I do, and I ask God to help and guide me.

The presiding minister addresses the assembly:
People of God, do you promise to support *these sisters and brothers*
and pray for *them* in *their* life in Christ?
We do, and we ask God to help and guide us.

BLESSING

PRAYER OF BLESSING

Those affirming baptism may kneel. The presiding minister continues:
Let us pray.
We give you thanks, O God,
that through water and the Holy Spirit
you give us new birth, wash us from sin,
and raise us to eternal life.
The following blessing may be repeated for each affirmer. The presiding minister may lay both
hands on the head of each person while speaking the blessing:
Stir up in <u>*name*</u> the gift of your Holy Spirit:
the spirit of wisdom and understanding,
the spirit of counsel and might,
the spirit of knowledge and the fear of the Lord,
the spirit of joy in your presence,
both now and forever.
Amen.

Parents, sponsors, mentors, or other representatives of the congregation may also offer a blessing.

ACCLAMATION

ACCLAMATION

The ministers and the affirmers face the assembly. A representative of the congregation addresses the assembly in these or similar words:
Let us give thanks for *those* affirming baptism
as we carry out the life of this Christian community
and its mission in the world.

The assembly addresses those affirming baptism:
As your sisters and brothers in the body of Christ,
we rejoice with you as you affirm your baptism.
Together let us give praise to God
and bear God's creative and redeeming word
to all the world.

BAPTISMAL REMEMBRANCE

This baptismal remembrance may be used to conclude the rite.

The presiding minister addresses the assembly in these or similar words:
When we were joined to Christ in the waters of baptism,
we were clothed with God's mercy and forgiveness.
Together let us remember our baptism.

The presiding minister gives thanks:
Blessed are you, O God of grace.
From age to age you made water a sign of your presence among us.
In the beginning your Spirit brooded over the waters
and you created the world by your word,
calling forth life in which you took delight.
You led Israel safely through the Red Sea into the land of promise,
and in the waters of the Jordan, you proclaimed Jesus your beloved one.
By water and the Spirit you adopted us as your daughters and sons,
making us heirs of the promise and servants of God.
Through this water remind us of our baptism.
Shower us with your Spirit,
that your forgiveness, grace, and love may be renewed in our lives.
To you be given honor and praise through Jesus Christ our Lord
in the unity of the Holy Spirit, now and forever.
Amen.

The acclamation may continue with a hymn, song, or psalm, during which the assembly may remember their baptism through a symbolic gesture: water from the font may be sprinkled upon the assembly, worshipers may touch the water and trace a sign of the cross upon themselves, or another appropriate action may be used.

At the conclusion of this action, the presiding minister addresses the assembly:
Almighty God,
who has given us a new birth by water and the Holy Spirit,
and bestowed on us the forgiveness of sins,
keep us in eternal life
through the grace of Jesus Christ our Lord.
Amen.

The liturgy continues with the intercessory prayers. Those affirming their baptism are included in the petitions.

AFFIRMATION of BAPTISM
Affirmation by the Assembly

This rite is intended for use on those occasions that call for an affirmation of the baptismal covenant by the whole assembly. Appropriate times for use include the Vigil of Easter, the Baptism of Our Lord, Sundays during the season of Easter, the Day of Pentecost, and All Saints Day. The rite may also be used in connection with significant occasions in the life of a congregation, such as a congregational anniversary.

Within the Sunday liturgy, at the conclusion of the hymn of the day, the ministers come to the font to lead the rite of affirmation. When space permits, the whole assembly may gather at the font.

PRESENTATION

PRESENTATION

The presiding minister addresses the assembly in these or similar words:
Dear friends, we give thanks to God for the gift of baptism
as we present ourselves before God this day
to affirm our baptism into Christ.
The presiding minister may note briefly the occasion for this affirmation.

PRAYER

The presiding minister may pray in these or similar words:
Let us pray.
Merciful God, we thank you that you have made us your own
by water and the word in baptism.
You have called us to yourself,
enlightened us with the gifts of your Spirit,
and nourished us in the community of faith.
Uphold your servants as we affirm the gifts and promises of baptism,
and unite the hearts of all whom you have brought to new birth
through this holy sacrament.
We ask this in the name of Christ.
Amen.

PROFESSION

RENUNCIATION OF EVIL

The presiding minister addresses the assembly:
As you affirm your baptism,
I ask you to reject sin, profess your faith in Christ, and confess the faith of the church.

Do you renounce the devil
   and all the forces that defy God?
I renounce them.

Do you renounce the powers of this world
   that rebel against God?
I renounce them.

Do you renounce the ways of sin
   that draw you from God?
I renounce them.

PROFESSION OF FAITH

The presiding minister may also say:
Do you turn to Christ as your Lord and Savior?
In faith I turn to Christ.

The presiding minister addresses the assembly:
With the whole church, let us confess our faith.

Do you believe in God the Father?
I believe in God, the Father almighty,
   creator of heaven and earth.

Do you believe in Jesus Christ, the Son of God?
I believe in Jesus Christ, God's only Son, our Lord,
   who was conceived by the Holy Spirit,
   born of the virgin Mary,
   suffered under Pontius Pilate,
   was crucified, died, and was buried;
   he descended to the dead.
On the third day he rose again;
   he ascended into heaven,
   he is seated at the right hand of the Father,
   and he will come to judge the living and the dead.

Do you believe in God the Holy Spirit?
I believe in the Holy Spirit,
   the holy catholic church,
   the communion of saints,
   the forgiveness of sins,
   the resurrection of the body,
   and the life everlasting. Amen.

COMMITMENT

You have made public profession of your faith.
Do you intend to continue in the covenant God made with you in holy baptism:
   to live among God's faithful people,
   to hear the word of God and share in the Lord's supper,
   to proclaim the good news of God in Christ through word and deed,
   to serve all people, following the example of Jesus,
   and to strive for justice and peace in all the earth?
I do, and I ask God to help and guide me.

BLESSING

PRAYER OF BLESSING

The presiding minister continues:
Let us pray.
We give you thanks, O God,
that through water and the Holy Spirit
you give us new birth,
wash us from sin,
and raise us to eternal life.
Stir up in each of us the gift of your Holy Spirit:
the spirit of wisdom and understanding,
the spirit of counsel and might,
the spirit of knowledge and the fear of the Lord,
the spirit of joy in your presence,
both now and forever.
Amen.

ACCLAMATION

BAPTISMAL REMEMBRANCE

The presiding minister addresses the assembly in these or similar words:
When we were joined to Christ in the waters of baptism,
we were clothed with God's mercy and forgiveness.
Together let us remember our baptism.

The presiding minister gives thanks:
Blessed are you, O God of grace.
From age to age you made water a sign of your presence among us.
In the beginning your Spirit brooded over the waters
and you created the world by your word,
calling forth life in which you took delight.
You led Israel safely through the Red Sea into the land of promise,
and in the waters of the Jordan, you proclaimed Jesus your beloved one.
By water and the Spirit you adopted us as your daughters and sons,
making us heirs of the promise and servants of God.
Through this water remind us of our baptism.
Shower us with your Spirit,
that your forgiveness, grace, and love may be renewed in our lives.
To you be given honor and praise through Jesus Christ our Lord
in the unity of the Holy Spirit, now and forever.
Amen.

*The acclamation may continue with a hymn, song, or psalm, during which the assembly may remember
their baptism through a symbolic gesture: water from the font may be sprinkled upon the assembly,
worshipers may touch the water and trace a sign of the cross upon themselves, or another appropriate
action may be used.*

At the conclusion of this action, the presiding minister addresses the assembly:
Almighty God,
who has given us a new birth by water and the Holy Spirit,
and bestowed on us the forgiveness of sins,
keep us in eternal life
through the grace of Jesus Christ our Lord.
Amen.

The liturgy continues with the intercessory prayers.

Formation in Faith

Related to Affirmation of Baptism

Shape of the Process

The church has often accompanied the celebration of affirmation of baptism in the worshiping assembly with a process of forming people in the Christian faith. Baptized people with a diverse range of experiences may seek life in a congregation or become interested in renewing their faith. They may affirm their baptism as a sign of their renewed participation in the life of the church or their entry into a particular congregation. Those who have been baptized at an early age often come through a period of nurture to an affirmation of baptism (sometimes called confirmation) in young adulthood. These persons may participate in catechesis and formation as they prepare for affirmation within a Christian community that is actively involved in the process of sharing the faith with them.

Formation in faith involves the whole person—body, mind, heart, and soul. Formation in the Christian faith takes place through worship, reflection on scripture, prayer, and ministry in daily life. Faith formation happens in different ways for each individual. It is a lifelong journey rather than a series of stages in faith development. The following pattern is similar to that used with people who are preparing for baptism. All or parts of it may assist congregations also in working with people who are preparing for affirmation of baptism.

As the process unfolds, liturgical rites that accompany this process of formation may be celebrated with the assembly to mark milestones along the way. These rites are indicated by italics in the following paragraphs and are presented in order following this description of the shape of the process.

INQUIRY

Inquiry is an open-ended period of time during which inquirers explore Christian faith and life. This period of inquiry is shaped by the needs of an inquirer as well as by parish leaders and the congregation. Through a public order of *Welcome of Inquirers*, inquirers are recognized by the congregation as people who are entering a period of deeper engagement with their faith. This welcome may be celebrated at any time during the church year.

AFFIRMATION

Affirmation is an open-ended period of time during which affirmers engage the Christian faith more deeply through the reading of scripture, prayer, worship, participation in word and sacrament, and ministry in daily life. This period of reflection and study may last from a few months to a number of years.

The process of affirmation is described at greater length in *What Do You Seek,* a guide for welcoming the adult inquirer. See the list of resources at the end of this volume.

When *Affirmation of Baptism* is to occur at Easter, Lent may be observed as a final period of preparation for candidates who will affirm their baptism at Easter. They may participate in *Call to Renewal* on Ash Wednesday, and an order of *Preparation for the Three Days* on Maundy Thursday. Together with candidates for baptism, they may also participate in one or more of the blessings on the Sundays in Lent (see pp. 37–50).

Affirmation of baptism may occur on a Sunday during the Easter season, at the Easter Vigil, or at any time throughout the church year. Since candidates for affirmation of baptism have already been baptized, they would ordinarily have been communicants since the time of inquiry.

BAPTISMAL LIVING

Even as formation in faith does not end with baptism, growth in the Christian faith and life does not conclude with an affirmation of baptism. An intentional time of reflection and study focused on baptismal living may follow and reinforce the occasion of affirmation. The fifty days of Easter offer one opportunity for this focus on the living of one's baptism both within the Christian community and in one's daily life beyond the church.

An order of *Affirmation of Christian Vocation* may be celebrated during which people who have participated in the process of affirmation may witness to particular ways in which they desire to live out their callings (vocations). For those who affirmed their baptism at Easter, it is particularly appropriate to celebrate this affirmation of vocation on the day of Pentecost; however, the rite may be used at any time.

WELCOME of INQUIRERS

Outline

GATHERING
Before the entrance hymn or after the prayer of the day:
Presentation

WORD
After the hymn of the day:
Signing with the Cross
Presentation of the Bible
Blessing
The Prayers

MEAL

SENDING

WELCOME of INQUIRERS

This welcome may be used whenever there are baptized people who desire to begin a more public relationship with a Christian congregation, or who are entering a particular period of formation leading to the affirmation of their baptism. This rite is intended to be used during the principal Sunday liturgy of the congregation.

PRESENTATION

At the door, before the entrance hymn, inquirers and their sponsors gather with the ministers. The assembly faces them. The presentation may also take place following the prayer of the day, in which case the inquirers and their sponsors may be invited to stand at their places or to stand before the presiding minister.

The presiding minister addresses the assembly:
Dear friends, we are gathered [at this door] today
to meet *these persons* who *have* been led by God's Spirit
to affirm *their* baptism into Christ.
Together, let us welcome *them* to this time of preparation and renewal.

A sponsor for each person says:
I present <u>name</u> to prepare for affirmation of baptism.

With these or similar words, the presiding minister asks each person presented:
What do you ask of God's church?
Response: To be strengthened in faith and renewed in the gift of baptism.

What do you seek from God's word?
Response: Faith and fullness of life.

The presiding minister continues:
Grace and mercy are given to all who call upon God's name.
We await your affirmation of baptism with joy.
Now I ask you, will you be faithful in learning the way of Christ?
Response: I will, and I ask God to help me.

The presiding minister addresses the sponsors and the assembly:
Sponsors, you now present *these persons* to us
in preparation for affirmation of baptism.
All of you who are assembled here are called to support
these sisters and brothers and *their sponsors*.
Will you help them hear the gospel of Christ
and be strengthened as members of the household of faith?
We will, and we ask God to help us.

The presiding minister continues:
Let us pray.
Merciful God,
we give you thanks for *name/s,*
whom you have made your own by water and the word in baptism.
You have called *them* today and *they have* answered you in our presence.
We praise you, O God, and we bless you.
We praise you, O God, and we bless you.

The assisting minister addresses the inquirers:
Now, *name/s,* come [into the church] and hear the word of God with us.

The liturgy continues with the entrance hymn. The inquirers and their sponsors may join the entrance procession and take their places in the assembly together.

SIGNING WITH THE CROSS

Following the hymn of the day, the inquirers and their sponsors gather before the assembly.

The presiding minister addresses the inquirers with these or similar words:
You have heard the holy and saving gospel of our Lord Jesus Christ.
Now receive the sign of that gospel, the sign given you in baptism,
on your body and in your heart,
that you may know the Lord and the power of his resurrection.

A sponsor traces a cross on the inquirer's forehead as the presiding minister says:
Receive the ☩ cross on your forehead,
a sign of God's endless love and mercy for you.
Learn to know and to follow Christ.

One of the following or another response may be sung or spoken by the congregation:

A

**Praise to you, O Christ,
the wisdom and power of God.**

B

**Glory and praise to you,
almighty and gracious God.**

The presiding minister may continue. A sponsor or catechist may trace a cross on each part of the inquirer's body as it is named.

Receive the ☩ cross on your ears,
that you may hear the gospel of Christ, the word of life. *Response*

Receive the ☩ cross on your eyes,
that you may see the light of Christ, illumination for your way. *Response*

Receive the ☩ cross on your lips,
that you may sing the praise of Christ, the joy of the church. *Response*

Receive the ☩ cross on your heart,
that God may dwell there by faith. *Response*

Receive the ☩ cross on your shoulders,
that you may bear the gentle yoke of Christ. *Response*

Receive the ☩ cross on your hands,
that God's mercy may be known in your work. *Response*

Receive the ☩ cross on your feet,
that you may walk in the way of Christ. *Response*

PRESENTATION OF THE BIBLE

A representative of the congregation presents a Bible to each inquirer with these or similar words:
Receive this Bible.
Hear God's word with us.
Learn and tell its stories.
Discover its mysteries.
Honor its commandments.
Rejoice in its good news.
May God's life-giving word, sweeter than honey,
inspire you and make you wise.

BLESSING

The inquirers may kneel. The presiding minister may extend both hands over the inquirers or may lay a hand on each inquirer's head during the prayer:
Let us pray.
Merciful and most high God,
creator and life-giver of all that is,
you have called all people
from darkness into light,
from error into truth,
from death into life.
We ask you:
Grant grace to *name/s* and bless *them*.
Raise *them* by your Spirit.
Revive *them* by your word.
Form *them* by your hand.
Renew in *them* the water of life
and feed *them* with the bread and cup of blessing,
that with all your people
they may bear witness to your grace
and praise you forever
through Jesus Christ our Lord.
Amen.

The assisting minister addresses the inquirers with these or similar words:
God bring you in peace and joy to fullness of life in Christ
and to the affirmation of your baptism.
Amen.

The inquirers and their sponsors return to their places. One of the following or another response may be sung or spoken by the assembly:

A

**May the God of all grace
who has called you to glory
support you and make you strong.**

B

**Blessed be God who chose you in Christ.
Live in love as Christ loved us.**

The liturgy continues with the intercessory prayers, which include petitions for those preparing to affirm their baptism and all who participate in the congregation's ministry of formation.

CALL to RENEWAL

Outline

GATHERING
Entrance Psalm or Hymn
Exhortation
Call to Renewal
Blessing
Confession of Sin
Imposition of Ashes
Prayer of the Day

WORD

MEAL

SENDING

CALL to RENEWAL

This rite may be used as part of the Ash Wednesday liturgy for those preparing to affirm their baptism at Easter. Prior to the confession and the imposition of ashes in the Ash Wednesday liturgy, those preparing for affirmation of baptism come forward with their sponsors.

EXHORTATION

The presiding minister may address the assembly with these or similar words:
Brothers and sisters in Christ,
on this Ash Wednesday the whole church enters a time of renewal
as it prepares to celebrate our Lord's passion, death, and resurrection.
Repentance, fasting, prayer, and works of love—the discipline of Lent—
help us engage in the spiritual struggle
against all that draws us away from God and our neighbor.
All who are in Christ are called to journey with Christ
by keeping a holy Lent.
Then, addressing those affirming baptism:
During this season, as you prepare to affirm your baptism,
you are called, with all the baptized,
to continuing renewal,
to die daily to sin,
and to walk in newness of life.

CALL TO RENEWAL

An assisting minister or other representative of the congregation says:
Name/s are preparing for affirmation of baptism and will continue *their* preparation
by joining with the entire congregation in keeping a holy Lent.

The presiding minister addresses the affirmers:
As you prepare to affirm the promises you made to God in baptism,
you stand among us as *examples* of the calling we all have
to walk in the ways of Christ.
Therefore I ask you, during this time of discipline and renewal:
Will you continue to hear the word of God
and receive it as a pattern for your *lives*?
Response: I will, with God's help.

Will you continue to deepen your life of prayer
for all God's people in Christ Jesus,
and for all people according to their needs?
Response: I will, with God's help.

Will you continue to join with the church in worship and service,
both in the community of faith and in the world,
by walking in love as Christ loved us and gave himself for us?
Response: I will, with God's help.

The presiding minister addresses the assembly with these or similar words:
People of God,
will you support and pray for these *sisters and brothers*
as *they* continue to prepare for baptismal affirmation?
We will, with God's help.

BLESSING

The presiding minister continues:
Let us pray.
Blessed are you, O Lord our God;
you have called your people
to do justice,
to love kindness,
and to walk humbly with you.
Bless *name/s* and all of your holy people
as we journey in faith this Lent.
Guide us to true repentance and renewal,
that we may follow in the way of the cross
of Jesus Christ, our Lord.
Amen.

The liturgy continues with the confession of sin, which may include the imposition of ashes. Those preparing for affirmation of baptism may be invited to receive the ashes, followed by the remaining persons in the assembly.

PREPARATION
for the THREE DAYS

Outline

GATHERING

WORD
After the hymn of the day:
Call to Service
Washing of Feet
The Prayers

MEAL

SENDING

PREPARATION for the THREE DAYS

This rite may be used on Maundy Thursday with those preparing to affirm their baptism at Easter.

Candidates for affirmation of baptism are encouraged to take part in individual confession and absolution at some time prior to the celebration of this rite.

When this rite is used, the appropriate gospel is John 13:1–17, 31b–35. Before the washing of feet in the Maundy Thursday liturgy, affirmers and their sponsors come forward and stand before the presiding minister.

CALL TO SERVICE

The presiding minister addresses the assembly:
Brothers and sisters in Christ:
On the night before his passion,
in an act of humble service,
Jesus knelt down and washed the feet of his friends.
In so doing he modeled a way of life for all of us who believe.

Jesus said, "I have set you an example,
that you should do as I have done to you."
No servant is greater than the master,
therefore, those who are disciples
readily accept such service from one another,
and continually model such service
in the ministry of their daily lives.

Then, addressing those preparing to affirm their baptism.
<u>Name/s,</u> you are preparing to affirm the covenant
God made with you in baptism.
We welcome you to join with the entire congregation
in dedicating *yourselves* anew to servant ministry,
to which all disciples of Jesus Christ have been called.

Tonight, we wash your feet as a sign of this servant ministry
and we ask that you in turn join us in this sign of discipleship.

WASHING OF FEET

The presiding minister washes the feet of the affirmers. After their feet have been washed, those affirming baptism receive basins, ewers, and towels to join in washing the feet of others in the assembly.

Appropriate hymns or songs may be sung by the assembly during the footwashing.

AFFIRMATION of CHRISTIAN VOCATION

Outline

GATHERING

WORD

MEAL

SENDING
Affirmation of Vocation
Blessing
Dismissal

AFFIRMATION of CHRISTIAN VOCATION

In preparation for this rite, it is important that those affirming Christian vocation be given adequate time to reflect on their place in the body of Christ and the vocation that they wish to affirm. Such preparation would certainly include reflection on how God's gifts of baptism, absolution, and communion shape the life of the Christian in the world.

The description of the area of service need not be extensive. The pastor and/or catechist may wish to assist in preparing this description. This is also a suitable project for discussion in the small groups with the catechist following affirmation of baptism.

When set within the liturgy of holy communion, this order is used to conclude the sending rite. The service may be adapted to other liturgical settings or other places within the liturgy.

AFFIRMATION OF VOCATION

Those affirming Christian vocation together with their sponsors gather with the ministers at the baptismal font.

The presiding minister addresses the assembly with these or similar words:
Dear Christian friends:
Baptized into the priesthood of Christ,
we are all called by the Holy Spirit
to offer ourselves to the Lord of all creation
in thanksgiving for all that God has done and continues to do for us.
It is our privilege to affirm those who are endeavoring
to carry out their vocation as Christians in the world.

A representative of the congregation says:
Through holy baptism God has set us free from sin
and made us members of the priesthood we share in Christ Jesus.
Through word and sacrament we have been nurtured in faith,
that we may give praise to God
and bear God's creative and redeeming word to all the world.

The assisting minister announces each name and a brief description of the area of service to be affirmed. Each person named may briefly comment on the significance of this choice.

The assembly may sing one of the following or another response after each person's comments:

A	B
May the God of all grace **who has called you to glory** **support you and make you strong.**	**Blessed be God who chose you in Christ.** **Live in love as Christ loved us.**

The presiding minister addresses those affirming their vocation:
<u>Name/s,</u> both your work and your rest are in God.
Will you endeavor to pattern your life on the Lord Jesus Christ,
in gratitude to God and in service to others,
at morning and evening, at work and at play,
all the days of your life?
Response: I will, and I ask God to help me.

Let us pray.
Almighty God,
by the power of the Spirit you have knit these your servants
into the one body of your Son, Jesus Christ.
Look with favor upon them in their commitment to serve in Christ's name.
Give them courage, patience, and vision;
and strengthen us all in our Christian vocation
of witness to the world and of service to others;
through Jesus Christ our Lord.
Amen.

BLESSING

The assisting minister addresses the assembly with these or similar words:
Go out into the world in peace;
be of good courage;
hold to what is good;
return no one evil for evil;
strengthen the faint-hearted;
support the weak;
help the suffering;
honor all people;
love and serve our God,
rejoicing in the power of the Holy Spirit.

The presiding minister blesses the assembly:
The almighty and merciful God, Father, ✝ Son, and Holy Spirit,
bless you now and forever.
Amen.

DISMISSAL

The assisting minister may dismiss the assembly:
Go in peace. Serve the Lord.
Thanks be to God.

Confession and Forgiveness

Shape of the Rite

In holy baptism, a person is joined to the saving death and resurrection of Jesus Christ and made a child of God forever. Washed in the water and marked with the cross, the newly-baptized is united not only with Christ, but also with other believers who together form a living community of faith.

Yet a profound paradox of the Christian life is that, although baptized and set free to live in love and faithfulness, human beings continue to sin and experience brokenness. The goodness of life can become distorted, human companionship strained, and our relationship with God shattered by the power of sin.

God promises, however, that life will be renewed and hope restored when sin is acknowledged and forgiveness embraced. In confession and forgiveness, honestly recognizing the sinfulness of human life, returning to the saving promises of God in baptism, the people of God are healed.

INVITATION
Hymn, Psalm, or Canticle
Opening Acclamation
Prayer of Preparation
Invitation

Whether brief or extended, corporate confession and forgiveness is a response to God's invitation to acknowledge our need for mercy. Song gathers the assembly into a common voice that praises God for the gifts of life, salvation, and resurrection from the dead. An acclamation of the God who creates and restores may be accompanied by the sign of the cross, made by all in remembrance of baptism. A prayer may follow, calling upon the Holy Spirit to guide and empower the assembly in its confession, and then the presiding minister invites all present to confess their sins before God and one another.

CONFESSION
Silence
Prayer of Confession

A period of silence helps people call to mind the many ways in which sin has scarred both personal and community life. After a period of reflection, the assembly acknowledges both communal and individual sin that is in need of forgiveness. This prayer of confession may take many forms, but it is always expansive enough to incorporate the experiences of the entire assembly.

FORGIVENESS
Declaration of Forgiveness
Laying On of Hands

The presiding minister declares that in Jesus Christ God forgives us all our sin. This forgiveness is not based on anything that an individual or assembly does, but on the mercy of God. Following this declaration of forgiveness, the presiding minister may lay hands on the head of each penitent, accompanied by an individual absolution and blessing.

ACCLAMATION
Hymn, Psalm, or Canticle
Thanksgiving for Water
Baptismal Remembrance
Peace

An acclamation may follow the declaration of forgiveness. Elements of the acclamation may include a song of praise and thanksgiving blessing God for the gift of forgiveness. In addition, the gifts of baptism may be remembered with a symbolic action involving water, such as the following: after a prayer of thanksgiving, water may be sprinkled upon the assembly, or worshipers may touch the water and trace a sign of the cross upon themselves. Finally, all who are present may greet one another with the peace of God.

CONFESSION and FORGIVENESS

Outline

INVITATION
Hymn, Psalm, or Canticle
Opening Acclamation
Prayer of Preparation
Invitation

CONFESSION
Silence
Prayer of Confession

FORGIVENESS
Declaration of Forgiveness
Laying On of Hands

ACCLAMATION
Hymn, Psalm, or Canticle
Thanksgiving for Water
Baptismal Remembrance
Peace

CONFESSION and FORGIVENESS
Brief Order

INVITATION

OPENING ACCLAMATION

As the presiding minister leads the acclamation, the sign of the cross may be made by all in remembrance of their baptism:

A

Praise to the blessed and holy ✛ Trinity,
one God,
who gives us life, salvation,
and resurrection.
Amen.

B

In the name of the Father,
and of the ✛ Son,
and of the Holy Spirit.
Amen.

p. 106 ▸

PRAYER OF PREPARATION

The presiding minister may continue, using one of the following or a similar prayer:

A

Almighty God,
to whom all hearts are open,
all desires known,
and from whom no secrets are hid:
Cleanse the thoughts of our hearts
by the inspiration of your Holy Spirit,
that we may perfectly love you
and worthily magnify your holy name,
through Jesus Christ our Lord.
Amen.

B

God of all mercy and consolation,
come to the aid of your people,
turning us from our sin
to live for you alone.
Give us the power of your Holy Spirit
that we may confess our sins,
receive your forgiveness,
and grow into the fullness of your Son,
Jesus Christ our Lord.
Amen.

p. 106 ▸

INVITATION

Using these or similar words, the presiding minister addresses the assembly:

A

God so loved the world
that while we were yet sinners
Jesus Christ was given to die for us.
Through the power of the Holy Spirit
God promises to heal us and forgive us.
Let us confess our sin
in the presence of God and of one another.

B

If we say we have no sin,
we deceive ourselves,
and the truth is not in us.
But if we confess our sins,
God who is faithful and just
will forgive our sins
and cleanse us from all unrighteousness.

p. 106 ▸

CONFESSION

Silence is kept for reflection.

PRAYER OF CONFESSION

A

Gracious God,
**have mercy on us.
In your compassion
forgive us our sins,
known and unknown,
things done and left undone.
Uphold us by your Spirit
so that we may live and serve you
in newness of life,
to the honor and glory
of your holy name;
through Jesus Christ our Lord.
Amen.**

B

Have mercy on us, O God,
**according to your lovingkindness.
In your great mercy,
wash away our iniquity
and cleanse us from our sin.
Create in us clean hearts, O God,
and renew a right spirit within us.
Do not cast us away from your presence,
nor take from us your Holy Spirit.
Restore to us the joy of your salvation
and give to us a willing spirit.
Amen.**

p. 107 ▸

FORGIVENESS

DECLARATION OF FORGIVENESS

The presiding minister addresses the assembly:

A

In the mercy of almighty God,
Jesus Christ was given to die for us,
and for his sake
God forgives us all our sins.
As a called and ordained minister
of the church of Christ and by his authority,
I therefore declare to you
the entire forgiveness of all your sins,
in the name of the Father,
and of the ✝ Son,
and of the Holy Spirit.
Amen.

B

The God of all mercy and consolation
has reconciled the world
through the death and resurrection
of Jesus Christ,
forgiving you all your sin.
By the power of the Holy Spirit
may the image of God be restored in you,
the wisdom of God renewed in you,
and the breath of God revived in you,
in the name of the blessed
and holy ✝ Trinity.
Amen.

p. 108 ▸

If this brief order is used prior to the liturgy of holy communion, the service continues with the entrance hymn. If the order is used after the prayers, the service continues with the greeting of peace.

CONFESSION and FORGIVENESS
Corporate Order

INVITATION

HYMN, PSALM OR CANTICLE

Psalm 25:1–17, Psalm 51:1–15, Psalm 103, another psalm, or an appropriate hymn or canticle
may be sung as the assembly gathers.

OPENING ACCLAMATION

As the presiding minister leads the acclamation, the sign of the cross may be made by all in remem-
brance of their baptism:

A

Praise to the blessed and holy ✛ Trinity,
one God,
who gives us life,
salvation, and resurrection.
Amen.

B   *p. 106* ►

In the name of the Father,
and of the ✛ Son,
and of the Holy Spirit.
Amen.

PRAYER OF PREPARATION

The presiding minister may continue, using one of the following or a similar prayer:

A

Almighty God,
to whom all hearts are open,
all desires known,
and from whom no secrets are hid:
Cleanse the thoughts of our hearts
by the inspiration of your Holy Spirit,
that we may perfectly love you
and worthily magnify your holy name,
through Jesus Christ our Lord.
Amen.

B   *p. 106* ►

God of all mercy and consolation,
come to the aid of your people,
turning us from our sin
to live for you alone.
Give us the power of your Holy Spirit
that we may confess our sins,
receive your forgiveness,
and grow into the fullness of your Son,
Jesus Christ our Lord.
Amen.

One or more readings from the scriptures may be proclaimed, including a reading from the gospels.
A homily may follow, or those present may participate in mutual conversation and consolation,
guided by the minister or another leader.

INVITATION

Using these or similar words, the presiding minister addresses the assembly:

p. 106 ▸

A

God so loved the world
that while we were yet sinners
Jesus Christ was given to die for us.
Through the power of the Holy Spirit
God promises to heal us and forgive us.
Let us confess our sin
in the presence of God and of one another.

B

If we say we have no sin,
we deceive ourselves,
and the truth is not in us.
But if we confess our sins,
God who is faithful and just
will forgive our sins
and cleanse us from all unrighteousness.

CONFESSION

Silence is kept for reflection.

PRAYER OF CONFESSION

C

p. 107 ▸

Most merciful God,
we confess that we are in bondage to sin and cannot free ourselves.
We have sinned against you in thought, word, and deed,
by what we have done and by what we have left undone.
We have not loved you with our whole heart;
we have not loved our neighbors as ourselves.
For the sake of your Son, Jesus Christ, have mercy on us.
Forgive us, renew us, and lead us,
so that we may delight in your will and walk in your ways,
to the glory of your holy name. Amen.

D

Gracious God,
our sins are too heavy to carry, too real to hide, and too deep to undo.
Forgive what our lips tremble to name,
what our hearts can no longer bear,
and what has become for us a consuming fire of judgment.
Set us free from a past that we cannot change;
open to us a future in which we can be changed;
and grant us grace to grow more and more in your likeness and image;
through Jesus Christ, the light of the world. Amen.

E

Holy God, holy and mighty, holy and immortal,
have mercy on us.

For boundless love of self,
and for failing to walk with humility and gentleness:
**Holy God, holy and mighty, holy and immortal,
have mercy on us.**

For longing to have what is not ours,
and for hearts that are not at rest with ourselves:
**Holy God, holy and mighty, holy and immortal,
have mercy on us.**

For misuse of human relationships,
and for unwillingness to see the image of God in others:
**Holy God, holy and mighty, holy and immortal,
have mercy on us.**

For jealousies that divide families and nations,
and for rivalries that create strife and warfare:
**Holy God, holy and mighty, holy and immortal,
have mercy on us.**

For inequity in sharing the gifts of God,
and for carelessness with the fruits of creation:
**Holy God, holy and mighty, holy and immortal,
have mercy on us.**

For hurtful words that condemn
and angry deeds that harm:
**Holy God, holy and mighty, holy and immortal,
have mercy on us.**

For idleness in witnessing to Jesus Christ,
and for squandering the gifts of love and grace:
**Holy God, holy and mighty, holy and immortal,
have mercy on us.**

FORGIVENESS

DECLARATION OF FORGIVENESS

The presiding minister addresses the assembly:

p. 108 ▶

C

In the mercy of almighty God
Jesus Christ was given to die for us,
and for his sake God forgives us all our sins.
Through the Holy Spirit we are cleansed
and given the power to proclaim
the mighty deeds of God
who called us out of darkness
into the splendor of light.
As a called and ordained minister of the
church of Christ and by his authority,
I therefore declare to you
the entire forgiveness of all your sins,
in the name of the Father,
and of the ☩ Son, and of the Holy Spirit.
Amen.

D

Jesus Christ our Savior
gave himself for us,
redeeming us from all sin
and cleansing us to be people
who are eager to do what is good.
Through the water of rebirth
and the outpouring of the Holy Spirit,
God saves us,
renews us in grace,
and bestows on us eternal life.
Amen.

LAYING ON OF HANDS

Those in the assembly may come forward and kneel.

The minister, laying both hands on each person's head, addresses each in turn:

A

In obedience to the command
of our Lord Jesus Christ,
I forgive you all your sins.
Amen.

B

The God of all mercy and consolation
forgive your sins,
strengthen you in all goodness,
and bring you to everlasting life.
Amen.

ACCLAMATION

HYMN, PSALM, OR CANTICLE

One of the following canticles, or another appropriate hymn or song may be sung:

A pp. 110–111 ▶

**Surely God is my salvation;
I will trust, and will not be afraid,
for the LORD GOD is my strength and my might;
he has become my salvation.
With joy you will draw water
from the wells of salvation.
And you will say in that day:
Give thanks to the LORD, call on his name;
make known his deeds among the nations;
proclaim that his name is exalted.
Sing praises to the LORD, for he has done gloriously;
let this be known in all the earth.
Shout aloud and sing for joy, O royal Zion,
for great in your midst is the Holy One of Israel.**

B

**Beloved, let us love one another,
for love is from God.
Everyone who loves is born of God and knows God;
whoever does not love does not know God,
for God is love.
In this is love,
not that we loved God but that God loved us
and sent the only Son to forgive our sins.
Beloved, since God so loved us,
let us also love one another.
For if we love one another,
God abides in us,
and the love of God is brought to fullness in us.**

THANKSGIVING FOR WATER

The presiding minister addresses the assembly in these or similar words:

A

In the waters of holy baptism
God liberates us
from the power of sin and death,
forever joining us
to the death and resurrection
of our Lord Jesus Christ.
May God's promise of everlasting life
be renewed in us
as we remember our baptism.

B

When we were joined to Christ
in the waters of baptism,
we were clothed
with God's mercy and forgiveness.
Together let us remember our baptism.

The presiding minister gives thanks:

A
pp. 108–110 ►

Blessed are you, O God of grace.
From age to age you made water a sign of your presence among us.
In the beginning your Spirit brooded over the waters
and you created the world by your word,
calling forth life in which you took delight.
You led Israel safely through the Red Sea into the land of promise,
and in the waters of the Jordan, you proclaimed Jesus your beloved one.
By water and the Spirit you adopted us as your daughters and sons,
making us heirs of the promise and servants of God.
Through this water remind us of our baptism.
Shower us with your Spirit,
that your forgiveness, grace, and love may be renewed in our lives.
To you be given honor and praise
through Jesus Christ our Lord,
in the unity of the Holy Spirit, now and forever.
Amen.

BAPTISMAL REMEMBRANCE

The assembly may remember their baptism through a symbolic gesture: water from the font may be sprinkled upon the assembly, worshipers may touch the water and trace a sign of the cross upon themselves, or another appropriate action may be used.

During the baptismal remembrance, the assembly may sing one of the following acclamations or an appropriate hymn, psalm, or canticle:

A

**You belong to Christ,
in whom you have been baptized.
Alleluia.
Alleluia.**

B p. 110 ▶

**Blessed be God,
the source of all life,
the word of salvation,
the spirit of mercy.**

The presiding minister addresses the assembly in these or similar words:
Almighty God,
who has given us a new birth by water and the Holy Spirit,
and bestowed on us the forgiveness of sins,
keep us in eternal life
though the grace of Jesus Christ our Lord.
Amen.

The liturgy concludes with the greeting of peace, prayers, the Lord's Prayer, and a blessing.

Or, if this service will include holy communion, the liturgy continues with the intercessory prayers.

REMEMBRANCE of BAPTISM

Outline

GATHERING
Entrance Hymn
Greeting
Thanksgiving for Water
Baptismal Remembrance
Prayer of the Day

WORD

MEAL

SENDING

GATHERING

WORD
After the hymn of the day:
Profession of Faith
Thanksgiving for Water
Baptismal Remembrance
The Prayers

MEAL

SENDING

REMEMBRANCE of BAPTISM

During the season of Easter and at other appropriate times throughout the year, a remembrance of baptism may be included in the liturgy of holy communion as an alternative to a brief order for confession and forgiveness. This remembrance may be part of the gathering rite, or it may follow the hymn of the day as part of the profession of faith.

AT THE GATHERING RITE

ENTRANCE HYMN

GREETING

Standing at the baptismal font, the presiding minister greets the assembly in these or similar words:

A

The grace and peace of Jesus Christ,
who was raised from the dead
to bring everlasting hope,
be with you all.
And also with you.

B

The blessed and holy Trinity,
one God,
who gives life, salvation, and resurrection,
be with you all.
And also with you.

THANKSGIVING FOR WATER

The presiding minister addresses the assembly in these or similar words:

A

In the waters of holy baptism
God liberates us
from the power of sin and death,
forever joining us to the death
and resurrection of our Lord Jesus Christ.
May God's promise of everlasting life
be renewed in us
as we remember our baptism.

B

When we were joined to Christ
in the waters of baptism,
we were clothed
with God's mercy and forgiveness.
Together let us remember our baptism.

The presiding minister gives thanks:

A

pp. 108–110 ►

Blessed are you, O God of grace.
From age to age you made water a sign of your presence among us.
In the beginning your Spirit brooded over the waters
and you created the world by your word,
calling forth life in which you took delight.
You led Israel safely through the Red Sea into the land of promise,
and in the waters of the Jordan, you proclaimed Jesus your beloved one.
By water and the Spirit you adopted us as your daughters and sons,
making us heirs of the promise and servants of God.
Through this water remind us of our baptism.
Shower us with your Spirit,
that your forgiveness, grace, and love may be renewed in our lives.
To you be given honor and praise through Jesus Christ our Lord
in the unity of the Holy Spirit, now and forever.
Amen.

BAPTISMAL REMEMBRANCE

The assembly may remember their baptism through a symbolic gesture: water from the font may be sprinkled upon the assembly, worshipers may touch the water and trace a sign of the cross upon themselves, or another appropriate action may be used.

During the baptismal remembrance, the assembly may sing one of the following hymns of praise, or another appropriate acclamation, hymn, or psalm focused on the remembrance of baptism:

C

pp. 110–111 ►

Glory to God in the highest,
and peace to God's people on earth.
Lord God, heavenly king,
almighty God and Father:
 we worship you, we give you thanks,
 we praise you for your glory.
Lord Jesus Christ,
only Son of the Father,
Lord God, Lamb of God:
you take away the sin of the world;
 have mercy on us.
You are seated at the right hand
 of the Father; receive our prayer.
For you alone are the Holy One,
you alone are the Lord,
you alone are the Most High,
 Jesus Christ, with the Holy Spirit,
 in the glory of God the Father.
 Amen.

D

This is the feast of victory for our God.
   Alleluia, alleluia, alleluia.
Worthy is Christ, the Lamb who was slain,
   whose blood set us free to be people of God.
Power, riches, wisdom, and strength,
   and honor, blessing, and glory are his.
Sing with all the people of God,
   and join in the hymn of all creation:
Blessing, honor, glory, and might be to God
   and the Lamb forever. Amen.
For the Lamb who was slain
   has begun his reign. Alleluia.
This is the feast of victory for our God.
   Alleluia, alleluia, alleluia.

The presiding minister addresses the assembly in these or similar words:
Almighty God,
who has given us a new birth by water and the Holy Spirit,
and bestowed on us the forgiveness of sins,
keep us in eternal life
through the grace of Jesus Christ our Lord.
Amen.

The liturgy continues with the prayer of the day.

AT THE PROFESSION OF FAITH

PROFESSION OF FAITH

Following the hymn of the day, the presiding minister stands at the baptismal font and addresses the assembly in these or similar words:
In the waters of holy baptism
God liberates us from the power of sin and death,
forever joining us to the death and resurrection of our Lord Jesus Christ.
With the whole church, let us confess our faith
as we remember our baptism.

Do you believe in God the Father?
**I believe in God, the Father almighty,
      creator of heaven and earth.**

Do you believe in Jesus Christ, the Son of God?
**I believe in Jesus Christ, God's only Son, our Lord,
      who was conceived by the Holy Spirit,
      born of the virgin Mary,
      suffered under Pontius Pilate,
      was crucified, died, and was buried;
      he descended to the dead.
On the third day he rose again;
      he ascended into heaven,
      he is seated at the right hand of the Father,
      and he will come to judge the living and the dead.**

Do you believe in God the Holy Spirit?
**I believe in the Holy Spirit,
      the holy catholic church,
      the communion of saints,
      the forgiveness of sins,
      the resurrection of the body,
      and the life everlasting. Amen.**

THANKSGIVING FOR WATER

The presiding minister gives thanks:

A

pp. 108–110 ►

Blessed are you, O God of grace.
From age to age you made water a sign of your presence among us.
In the beginning your Spirit brooded over the waters
and you created the world by your word,
calling forth life in which you took delight.
You led Israel safely through the Red Sea into the land of promise,
and in the waters of the Jordan, you proclaimed Jesus your beloved one.
By water and the Spirit you adopted us as your daughters and sons,
making us heirs of the promise and servants of God.
Through this water remind us of our baptism.
Shower us with your Spirit,
that your forgiveness, grace, and love may be renewed in our lives.
To you be given honor and praise through Jesus Christ our Lord
in the unity of the Holy Spirit, now and forever.
Amen.

BAPTISMAL REMEMBRANCE

*The assembly may remember their baptism through a symbolic gesture: water from the font may be
sprinkled upon the assembly, worshipers may touch the water and trace a sign of the cross upon
themselves, or another appropriate action may be used.*

*During the baptismal remembrance, the assembly may sing one of the following acclamations, or
another appropriate hymn or psalm:*

A

B

p. 110 ►

You belong to Christ,
in whom you have been baptized.
Alleluia.
Alleluia.

Blessed be God,
the source of all life,
the word of salvation,
the spirit of mercy.

The presiding minister addresses the assembly in these or similar words:
Almighty God,
who has given us a new birth by water and the Holy Spirit,
and bestowed on us the forgiveness of sins,
keep us in eternal life
through the grace of Jesus Christ our Lord.
Amen.

The liturgy continues with the intercessory prayers.

Supplemental Materials

OPENING ACCLAMATION

C

Blessed be the God of our salvation,
who bears our burdens and ✝ forgives our sins.
Amen.

PRAYER OF PREPARATION

C

Eternal God, in whom we live
and move and have our being,
whose face is hidden from us by our sins,
and whose mercy we forget
in the blindness of our hearts:
Cleanse us from all our offenses,
and deliver us from proud thoughts
and vain desires,
that with reverent and humble hearts
we may draw near to you,
confessing our faults,
confiding in your grace,
and finding in you our refuge and strength;
through Jesus Christ our Lord.
Amen.

INVITATION

C

Since we have such a great high priest
who has passed through the heavens,
Jesus Christ our Lord,
let us with confidence draw near to God
that we may receive mercy
and find grace in time of need.

PRAYER OF CONFESSION

F

God of all mercy,
we confess that we have sinned against you,
opposing your will in our lives.
We have denied your goodness in each other,
in ourselves, and in the world you have created.
We repent of the evil that enslaves us,
the evil we have done,
and the evil done on our behalf.
Forgive, restore, and strengthen us
through our Savior Jesus Christ,
that we may abide in your love and serve only your will. Amen.

G

Almighty and merciful God,
I, a troubled and penitent sinner,
confess to you all my sins and iniquities
with which I have offended you
and for which I justly deserve your punishment.
I am sorry for them, and repent of them,
and pray for your boundless mercy.
For the sake of the suffering and death of your Son, Jesus Christ,
be gracious and merciful to me, a poor sinful being;
forgive my sins,
give me your Holy Spirit for the amendment of my sinful life,
and bring me to life everlasting. Amen.

H

Merciful God,
we have sinned against heaven and against you,
and are not worthy to be called your children.
Have mercy on us and turn us from our sinful ways.
Bring us back to you
as those who once were dead but now have life,
through Jesus Christ our Lord. Amen.

DECLARATION OF FORGIVENESS

E

Almighty God have mercy on you,
forgive you all your sins
through the grace of ✝ Jesus Christ,
strengthen you in all goodness,
and by the power of the Holy Spirit
keep you in eternal life.
Amen.

F

The Lord is gracious and full of compassion,
slow to anger and abounding in steadfast love.
To all who believe in Jesus Christ
God grants freedom from the power of sin,
and through the Holy Spirit
gives life, forgiveness, and resurrection from the dead.
Amen.

THANKSGIVING FOR WATER

B

All-powerful and ever-living God,
your gift of water brings life and freshness to the earth;
by water we are cleansed from sin and receive eternal life.
Renew in us the living fountain of your grace
and defend us, soul and body, from evil,
that we may approach you with pure hearts
and worthily receive your gift of salvation.
We ask this through Jesus Christ our Lord.
Amen.

C

Blessed are you, holy God.
You are the creator of the waters of the earth.
You are the river of life.
You led your people through the river Jordan
and called them to life in covenant.
Your Son was baptized in the river Jordan
to begin his mission among us.
Through this water remind us of our baptism.
Create us all anew
that we may serve this needy world;
for we trust in the name of Jesus, your Son,
who lives with you and the Holy Spirit,
one God, now and forever.
Amen.

D

Holy God, holy and merciful, holy and mighty,
you are the river of life,
you are the everlasting wellspring,
you are the fire of rebirth.
Glory to you for oceans and lakes, for rivers and creeks.
Honor to you for cloud and rain, for dew and snow.
Your waters are below us, around us, above us:
our life is born in you.
You are the fountain of resurrection.
Praise to you for your saving waters:
Noah and the animals survive the flood,
Hagar discovers your well.
The Israelites escape through the sea,
and they drink from your gushing rock.
Naaman washes his leprosy away,
and the Samaritan woman will never be thirsty again.
At this font, holy God, we pray.
Through this water remind us of our baptism.
Illumine our days.
Enliven our bones.
Dry our tears.
Wash away the sin within us,
and drown the evil around us.
Satisfy all our thirst with your eternal fountain,
and bring to birth the body of Christ,
who lives with you and the Holy Spirit,
one God, now and forever.
Amen.

E

Blessed are you, holy God.
You are the creator of the waters of the earth.
You are the fire of rebirth.
You poured out your Spirit on your people Israel.
You breathe life into our dry bones.
Your Son promised to send the Spirit to us
that the world may know your peace and truth.
Through this water remind us of our baptism.
As your beloved children
may we embody your Spirit in the world;
for we call on the name of your Son,
who lives with you and the Holy Spirit,
one God, now and forever.
Amen.

F

Blessed are you, holy God.
You are the creator of the waters of the earth.
You are the everlasting wellspring.
You gather your people from sea to sea.
You quench our thirst, and you comfort all who weep.
Your Son stands among us, Shepherd and Lamb,
to lead all the saints through death to life.
Through this water remind us of our baptism.
May this water be a sign of the end of all tears;
for we stand under the name above every name, Jesus your Son,
who lives with you and the Holy Spirit,
one God, now and forever.
Amen.

ACCLAMATION

C

Blessed be God,
who chose you in Christ.
Live in love as Christ loved us.

HYMNS, PSALMS, AND CANTICLES

E

Blessed be the God and Father of our Lord Jesus Christ,
by whose great mercy we have new birth into a living hope;
through the resurrection of Jesus Christ from the dead,
we have an inheritance that is imperishable in heaven.
The ransom that was paid to free us
was not paid in silver or gold,
but the precious blood of Christ,
the Lamb without spot or stain.
God raised Jesus from the dead and gave him glory
so that we might have faith and hope in God.

F

Refrain

Springs of water, bless the Lord.
Give God glory and praise forever.

Verses

Buried with Christ in death, you are raised with him to life.

Bathed in the fountain of life, you are born to a living hope.

You are God's work of art, created in Christ Jesus.

You belong to Christ, in whom you have been baptized.

All of you are one, united in Christ Jesus.

Rejoice, all you baptized, called to be children of God.

Additional options may include hymns and songs such as the following:
We know that Christ is raised   LBW 189
Jesus Christ, my sure defense   LBW 340
Guide me ever, great Redeemer   LBW 343
I'm so glad Jesus lifted me   TFF 191
This joyful Eastertide   WOV 676
Shall we gather at the river   WOV 690
O blessed spring   WOV 695
We were baptized in Christ Jesus   WOV 698
Baptized and set free   WP 14
Song over the waters   WP 127
Waterlife   WP 145

Acknowledgments

Holy Baptism and Related Rites editorial team: Dennis Bushkofsky, Sarah Henrich, Paul Hoffman, Mary Hughes; Michael Burk, Cheryl Dieter, Martin A. Seltz, Frank Stoldt (Renewing Worship project management staff).

Holy Baptism and Related Rites development panel: Nancy Amacher, Daniel Benedict, Susan Briehl, Lorraine Brugh, Joseph Donnella II, Norma Cook Everist, Jill Higgins Hendrix, Robert Hofstad, Donald Johnson, Maxwell Johnson, Thomas K. Johnson, Gordon Lathrop, Rafael Malpica-Padilla, Katherine S. Miller, Jeffrey S. Nelson, John Nunes, Elsa Quanbeck, Gail Ramshaw, Robert A. Rimbo, Nelson Rivera, Jan A. Ruud Sr., Craig Satterlee, Thomas H. Schattauer, Jeffrey C. Silleck, Jeffrey A. Truscott, Karen Walhof.

Design and production: Jessica Hillstrom, Linda Parriott, Eric Vollen, production; Carolyn Porter of The Kantor Group, Inc., book design; Nicholas Markell, logo design.

The material on pages i–111 is covered by the copyright of this book. Unless otherwise noted, the material has been prepared by the editorial team. Material from the sources listed here is gratefully acknowledged and is used by permission. Every effort has been made to identify the copyright administrators for copyrighted texts. The publisher regrets any oversight that may have occurred and will make proper acknowledgment in future editions if correct information is brought to the publisher's attention.

Scripture quotations, unless otherwise noted, are from the New Revised Standard Version Bible © 1989 Division of Christian Education of the National Council of Churches of Christ in the United States of America. Used by permission.

Commissioned texts prepared by Gail Ramshaw, © 2002 Augsburg Fortress: baptism acclamation B, 9, 99, 105; baptism thanksgivings E–H, 16–18; remembrance of baptism thanksgivings C–F, 108–110

Book of Common Prayer (1979) of the Episcopal Church USA: prayer of confession A, 92; declaration of forgiveness E, 108

Book of Common Worship, © 1993 Westminster John Knox Press: baptism thanksgiving C, 14; prayer of confession D, 94

Common Worship: Services and Prayers for the Church of England, © 2000 The Archbishops' Council: renunciation of evil C, 12

Enriching Our Worship 1, © 1998 The Church Pension Fund: confession opening acclamation C, 106; prayer of confession F, 107

Living Witnesses: The Adult Catechumenate, © 1992 Evangelical Lutheran Church in Canada: selected materials included and revised in *Welcome to Christ: Lutheran Rites for the Catechumenate.*

Lutheran Book of Worship, © 1978, administered by Augsburg Fortress: signing with the cross, 9; baptism introduction C, 11; questions to parents and sponsors, adapt., 11; baptism thanksgiving B, adapt., 13; presentation of a candle B, 18; affirmation commitment, adapt., 57, 62, 67; prayer of confession C, 94; "This is the feast of victory," 103; prayer of confession G, 107

A New Zealand Prayer Book / He Karakia Mihinare o Aotearoa, © 1989 The Anglican Church in Aotearoa, New Zealand and Polynesia: presentation of a candle A, 10

Praying Together, © 1988 English Language Liturgical Consultation (ELLC): Apostles' Creed, 7, 12, 36, 56, 61, 66; thanksgiving dialogue, 8; "Glory to God in the highest," 102

This Far by Faith: An African American Resource for Worship, © 1999 Augsburg Fortress: baptism thanksgiving D, 15; prayer of confession B, 92

Welcome to Christ: Lutheran Rites for the Catechumenate, © 1997 Augsburg Fortress, adapt.: baptism acclamations C and D, 18, 110; Welcome of Inquirers, 24–29; Enrollment of Candidates for Baptism, 30–33; Blessing of Candidates for Baptism, 34–47; Affirmation of the Vocation of the Baptized in the World, 48–50; remembrance of baptism acclamation F, 111

What Do You Seek?: Welcoming the Adult Inquirer, © 2000 Augsburg Fortress, adapt.; Welcome of Inquirers, 72–77; Calling of the Baptized to Continuing Renewal, 78–80; Preparation for the Three Days, 82–83; Affirmation of the Vocation of the Baptized in the World, 84–86

With One Voice, © 1995 Augsburg Fortress: confession prayer of preparation B, 91–93; declaration of forgiveness A, 92

Worship 99, © 1999 Evangelical Lutheran Church in America: acclamation/thanksgiving for water A, 51, 63, 68, 98, 102, 105

For Further Reading

BAPTISM

Baptism and the Unity of the Church, eds. Michael Root and Risto Saarinen. Grand Rapids: Wm. B. Eerdmans and World Council of Churches, 1998.

> While the churches are divided on the meaning of the unity of the church, they recognize the value of their common baptism. This diverse collection of essays frames the essential questions and issues in the discussion of baptism and ecclesial communion.

Johnson, Maxwell E., ed. *Living Water, Sealing Spirit: Readings on Christian Initiation.* Collegeville, Minnesota: Pueblo Books, 1995.

> This is a collection of essays on a wide range of topics relating to baptism and confirmation written by a variety of contemporary scholars of liturgical theology and history. The volume would be a good beginning for anyone who is trying to understand some of the major issues in contemporary thought relating to baptism.

Kuehn, Regina. *A Place for Baptism.* Chicago: Liturgy Training Publications, 1992.

> This work explores the meaning of baptism through the design of baptisteries. Many styles, old and new, are pictured and examined.

Ramshaw-Schmidt, Gail. "Celebrating Baptism in Stages: A Proposal." In *Alternative Futures for Worship.* Vol. 2: *Baptism and Confirmation,* ed. Mark Searle. Collegeville: The Liturgical Press, 1987.

> Gail Ramshaw presents a proposal for the celebration of infant baptism in stages, using the Roman Catholic Church's *Rite of Christian Initiation of Adults* (RCIA) as a model. Parents are supported during the months before birth and in the weeks between birth and the actual baptism. The author also calls all the baptized to a continuing renewal and remembrance of baptism.

AFFIRMATION OF BAPTISM

Browning, Robert L. and Roy A. Reed. *Models of Confirmation and Baptismal Affirmation.* Birmingham, Alabama: Religious Education Press, 1995.

> This is an ecumenical study that examines the established and emerging pastoral patterns of confirmation in seven denominations. The writers suggest that confirmation and the reaffirmation of baptism are repeatable rites in an individual's life. The educational and liturgical issues are addressed with recommendations for ministry with five age groups from infants to older adults, while including sample worship rites for the entire life span.

Confirmation: Engaging Lutheran Foundations and Practices. Minneapolis: Augsburg
Fortress, 1999.

> In this volume, nine leading Lutheran scholars examine the theological, historical and
> educational foundations of confirmation ministry in the ELCA. This book identifies
> the key issues and concerns of today's confirmation ministry planners and deepens the
> educators' commitment to teaching the Lutheran faith to people of all ages—especially
> adolescents—in a way that is gospel and grace-centered.

Johnson, Thomas K. *Confirmation: A Congregational Planner.* Minneapolis: Augsburg
Fortress, 1999.

> This book offers a brief background about the history and theology of confirmation,
> but its main purpose is for congregational teams to use in designing confirmation pro-
> grams that will be most effective in their own contexts.

CONFESSION AND FORGIVENESS

Müller-Fahrenholz, Geiko. *The Art of Forgiveness: Theological Reflections on Healing
and Reconciliation.* Geneva: WCC Publications, 1997.

> This book grows out of the conviction that, as the author says, "it is necessary to think
> about forgiveness not in spite of Auschwitz but because of Auschwitz." Drawing on
> the biblical tradition and church history, Geiko Müller-Fahrenholz shows how the idea
> of forgiveness has been distorted, abused and largely lost, and why it is of ultimate im-
> portance to reclaim this healing art, not only in personal relations but especially also in
> the relations between nations and peoples.

A Reconciliation Sourcebook, comps. Kathleen Hughes and Joseph A. Favazza. Chicago:
Liturgy Training Publications, 1997.

> The experience of alienation and reconciliation is fundamentally human. For this rea-
> son, no individual field of study can adequately contain it. This *Reconciliation Source-
> book* contains a wide range of texts that attempt to give insight from a variety of cul-
> tural and disciplinary perspectives. The familiar parable of the Prodigal Son is the
> framework for the texts, which are organized around ten themes, from division and
> alienation through penance, mercy, and celebration.

CATECHUMENATE

Catechumenate. Liturgy Training Publications, Chicago.

> This journal of Christian initiation, published six times a year, is intended primarily
> for parish leaders, lay and ordained, who prepare persons for the rites of the catechu-
> menate. Most of the authors are nationally recognized leaders in liturgy and the cate-
> chumenate, and they bring a wealth of experience to their articles.

This Is the Night. Chicago: Liturgy Training Publications, 1992. VHS cassette, 30 minutes.
This video presents actual footage of rites of the adult catechumenate as they have been conducted in a Roman Catholic parish in Pasadena, Texas. Personal observations are included by parish members and adult baptismal candidates themselves. The video demonstrates the use of a baptismal immersion font, and how water and other elements can serve as more complete signs of sacramental action.

Welcome to Christ: A Lutheran Catechetical Guide. Minneapolis: Augsburg Fortress, 1997.
This volume offers practical advice on the foundations of ministry to the newcomer: scripture study, personal prayer and communal worship, and ministry in daily life. An annotated bibliography presents Lutheran and ecumenical resources that will help congregations carry out this baptismal ministry.

Welcome to Christ: A Lutheran Introduction to the Catechumenate. Minneapolis: Augsburg Fortress, 1997.
This volume explores the cultural, pastoral, and theological aspects of welcoming adults to Christ and the Christian community. A one-page chart provides an overview of the catechumenal process, along with the liturgical rites that are central to it.

Welcome to Christ: Lutheran Rites for the Catechumenate. Minneapolis: Augsburg Fortress, 1997.
Orders of worship and prayers throughout the four times of the catechumenate are presented: Welcome of Inquirers, Prayers of Encouragement, Enrollment of Candidates for Baptism, Blessing of Candidates for Baptism, Baptism and Communion at the Vigil of Easter, Affirmation of the Vocation of the Baptized in the World. Reproducible music for the rites, which can also be used for many of the responses and acclamations in *Holy Baptism and Related Rites*, is included in an appendix.

Welcome to Christ: Preparing Adults for Baptism and Discipleship Videotape; Chicago: Evangelical Lutheran Church in America, 1998. VHS cassette, 20 minutes.
This video in the Welcome to Christ series teaches the basics of the catechumenal process by telling the stories of two Lutheran congregations in the Pacific Northwest that use catechumenal ministry (integrating faith formation, worship, evangelism, and social action).

What Do You Seek?: Welcoming the Adult Inquirer. Minneapolis: Augsburg Fortress, 2000.
A collection of essays on ministry to, and reception of, new members and those reaffirming their baptism in congregations, with resources for small groups and public worship.

GENERAL REFERENCE

The Use of the Means of Grace: A Statement on the Practice of Word and Sacrament.
Evangelical Lutheran Church in America. Minneapolis: Augsburg Fortress, 1997.
> The Renewing Worship series is based on this statement's foundation. While the state-
> ment provides much needed guidance on basic worship matters for Lutheran congre-
> gations and their leaders, it may also be used as a document for general reference and
> for congregational studies.

RENEWING WORSHIP

A series of provisional resources produced by the Evangelical Lutheran Church in America
as part of the Renewing Worship multiyear project to prepare new primary worship resources. Each includes the opportunity for feedback and response.

Congregational Song: Proposals for Renewal. Renewing Worship, vol. 1. Minneapolis:
Augsburg Fortress, 2001.
> Over eighty hymns, many of them reproducible for use in congregational bulletins,
> present various strategies for the renewal and revision of the treasured tradition of the
> church's song.

Principles for Worship. Renewing Worship, vol. 2. Minneapolis: Augsburg Fortress, 2002.
> Guiding principles for language, music, preaching, and worship space, developed
> through a churchwide consultative process. The principles, with their supporting back-
> ground and applications, are based upon the content and the model of *The Use of the
> Means of Grace,* which is included in full as an appendix.

Forthcoming volumes in the series (projected dates, subject to change):

Life Passages: Marriage, Healing, Funeral. Renewing Worship, vol. 4 (2002).

New Hymns and Songs. Renewing Worship, vol. 5 (2003).

Holy Communion and Related Rites. Renewing Worship, vol. 6 (2004).

Daily Prayer. Renewing Worship, vol. 7 (2004).

The Church's Year: Propers and Seasonal Rites. Renewing Worship, vol. 8 (2004).

Ministry and the Church's Life. Renewing Worship, vol. 9. (2005).

Evaluation

An essential goal of Renewing Worship is the use of provisional resources in worship and the evaluation of these resources by congregations and their leaders. Some congregations may use only a few of the rites in this volume, while others may use most or all of them. Included here as well as at www.renewingworship.org is a reproducible evaluation tool that can be used to evaluate any or all of the rites contained in *Holy Baptism and Related Rites.*

Evaluations for different rites may be submitted together or individually, at one time or over the course of several years, but please fill out a separate form for each rite. Be sure to include the completed last page of the evaluation with each submission.

Please place a check mark next to the rite you are evaluating (choose one rite only for each form):

Holy Baptism
_____ Holy Baptism

Formation in Faith Related to Baptism
_____ Welcome of Inquirers
_____ Enrollment of Candidates for Baptism
_____ Blessing of Candidates: Confession of Faith
_____ Blessing of Candidates: Renunciation of Evil
_____ Blessing of Candidates: Commitment to Prayer
_____ Affirmation of Christian Vocation

Affirmation of Baptism
_____ Public Profession of Faith
_____ Confirmation
_____ Affirmation by the Assembly

Formation in Faith Related to Affirmation of Baptism
_____ Welcome of Inquirers
_____ Call to Renewal
_____ Preparation for the Three Days
_____ Affirmation of Christian Vocation

Confession and Forgiveness
_____ Confession and Forgiveness: Brief Order
_____ Confession and Forgiveness: Corporate Order
_____ Remembrance of Baptism

Please indicate your agreement with the statements that follow by circling the appropriate number. If desired, add comments to support your response.

1. The rite is faithful to scripture and the church's tradition.

Agree				Disagree
1	2	3	4	5

Comments:

2. The style and language of the rite is accessible to our worshiping assembly.

Agree				Disagree
1	2	3	4	5

Comments:

3. The rite is easy to follow and to adapt for our worshiping assembly.

Agree				Disagree
1	2	3	4	5

Comments:

4. The rite is useful in the life of our congregation.

Agree				Disagree
1	2	3	4	5

Comments:

5. Who was involved in the planning related to use of this rite?

_____ Pastor(s)
_____ Pastor(s) and other staff
_____ Group of lay members with pastoral and other staff
_____ Other (describe): _____

6. In what context was the rite used?

_____ Within a regularly scheduled service of Holy Communion
_____ Within a regularly scheduled Service of the Word
_____ Within another type of regularly scheduled service
_____ Outside of a regularly scheduled service
_____ Studied but not used in worship

7. How many times did you use the rite prior to this evaluation? _____

8. One of the goals of Renewing Worship is to provide options that can be used in flexible ways. Which statement best describes the options provided in this rite?

_____ A sufficient number of options are provided with the rite.
_____ Too many options are provided with the rite.
_____ Too few options are provided with the rite.

9. Are there additional rites related to the rites in *Holy Baptism and Related Rites* that should be included in final resources? Please describe.

10. Please note any additional comments and suggestions for improvement.

INFORMATION ABOUT THIS EVALUATION

Please provide the requested information and include it with each separately submitted evaluation, whether filled in on this form (or a photocopy of it) or in a letter.

ELCA Congregation ID # _____

If this response is not from an ELCA congregation or you do not know your congregation ID number, please note:
    Congregation: _____
    Location: _____
    Denomination: _____

Who prepared this evaluation?
Name: _____

I am: _____ Female _____ Male
I am: _____ Lay _____ Lay-rostered _____ Congregational pastor
    _____ Pastor in specialized ministry/retired
I am: _____ Paid staff _____ Volunteer staff _____ Not staff
I am: _____ American Indian or Alaska Native
    _____ Black or African American
    _____ Hispanic or Latino/a
    _____ Native Hawaiian or other Pacific Islander
    _____ White
    _____ Other: _____

I am: _____ Under 25 _____ 25–50 _____ 50–65 _____ over 65

Is this _____ a personal evaluation of the rites _____ a response to which a group has agreed?

Have you been part of a group that studied or discussed these rites? _____ Yes _____ No

What is the nature of this group?
    _____ Congregation council or other congregational leadership
    _____ Congregational study group made up primarily of lay people
    _____ Group of congregational pastors and/or other rostered leaders
    _____ Other (describe): _____

Please return the completed evaluation to Renewing Worship Evaluation, Division for Congregational Ministries, Evangelical Lutheran Church in America, 8765 West Higgins Road, Chicago, IL 60631.

—